# Praise for *Straight-A Study Skills*

"I'm so proud that Cindy, a former intern of mine, and he
young people reach their academic and personal potentia..

—U.S. Senator Barbara Boxer

"The Muchnicks' book is a thoughtful and thorough guide to ways in which student behavior can be changed for the better. I have no doubt that any student who takes their recommendations seriously will learn better, be a more successful student, and productively apply these lessons to all of life's work."

—Ted O'Neill, Former Dean of Admissions and Current Lecturer
in Humanities in the College of the University of Chicago

"I loved getting a chance to go through [this] book. It is truly chock full of great advice for students at every level who want to get the most out of school, and who want to prepare well for the next step in their education. It provides a valuable service to students, parents, and teachers by encouraging students to take responsibility for their learning. I really like that; it puts responsibility where it belongs—with the student and how he or she approaches learning on a very practical level. There's a lot here—too much probably for any one student or family to fully absorb. There are hundreds of pieces of good advice, and I expect parents and children will end up highlighting a dozen or so that they want to focus on. Taking even some of this advice to heart, and acting on it, will help any student get more out of school. This could well be one of those books parents and students return to over and over again, to be reminded of the many ways to approach their schooling well."

—Christoph Guttentag, Dean of Undergraduate Admissions at Duke University

"This book is essential reading for students who want practical advice and a strategic plan for achieving success in the classroom and beyond. Whether you are in middle school, high school, or college, *Straight-A Study Skills* provides insights and strategies that will help you to become the best student you can be."

—Jody Maxmin, Associate Professor of Art History
and Classics at Stanford University

# Praise for *Straight-A Study Skills*

"*Straight-A Study Skills* provides clear, concise, and powerful tips for student success both inside and outside the classroom."

—Bill Coplin, Professor of Public Affairs, Maxwell School, Syracuse University (*www.bill.coplin.org*)

"The life of a student in our increasingly technological and global world is growing more complex with every passing year. Written by the mother-and-son team of Cynthia and Justin Muchnick, one of our Phillips Academy students, this book is a helpful how-to guide for young people and their parents wishing to cut through the clutter. The Muchnicks offer hundreds of specific tips and general good sense, which should prove useful to a generation of learners seeking to make the most of their education."

—John Palfrey, Head of School, Phillips Academy

# STRAIGHT-A
# STUDY
# SKILLS

More Than **200** Essential Strategies
to Ace Your Exams, Boost Your Grades,
and ACHIEVE LASTING ACADEMIC SUCCESS

Cynthia Clumeck Muchnick, MA,
and Justin Ross Muchnick

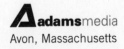
**A**adamsmedia
Avon, Massachusetts

Published by
Adams Media, a division of F+W Media, Inc.
57 Littlefield Street, Avon, MA 02322. U.S.A.
*www.adamsmedia.com*

ISBN 10: 1-4405-5246-0
ISBN 13: 978-1-4405-5246-5
eISBN 10: 1-4405-5247-9
eISBN 13: 978-1-4405-5247-2

# DEDICATION

*From Cindy:* To Adam, Justin, Jacob, Ross, and Ally. You all complete me.

*From Justin:* For my family.

# ACKNOWLEDGMENTS

*From Cindy:* This book could not have been possible without the help of my dedicated coauthor and son, Justin. I am pretty sure this is my most well-written book to date! Thank you for the keen eye, academic insights, and grammatical precision that you brought to this effort. I have a feeling this will be the first of many published books in your future! I loved sharing this project with you. We had a lot of laughs. Thanks to Jacob, Ross, and Ally for your patience as Justin and I worked late into the night. We hope the ideas in this book will help all of you in school! Adam, thank you for your constant love and support. Thank you to my devoted literary agent, Grace Freedson, for bringing me this project and Ross Weisman and Peter Archer at Adams Media for editing our words and moving this project along. And to my parents, thank you for always believing in me.

*From Justin:* Many thanks to my grandparents, parents, and siblings for all of their guidance and support through the years.

# CONTENTS

# THE PURPOSE OF SCHOOL AND HOW TO MASTER IT

This book promises easy-to-digest concepts, techniques, and tactics to help you achieve academic success. Read the book with a highlighter and focus on the skills you want to master. Use the ideas contained within to inspire you to practice new approaches. Try tweaking your learning style to see if you can improve in the classroom. Read these ideas and apply them immediately. Here are some basic ways to be successful in school:

»   Treat school as your job.
»   Pursue learning with passion, vigor, and an open mind.
»   Always attend class. Arrive on time and ready to learn.

- » Do your homework and extra-credit options.
- » Set academic, extracurricular, and social goals and aim to achieve them.
- » Become an active learner, a good listener, and class participant. Think outside the box and strive to make interdisciplinary connections among your various classes.
- » Demonstrate responsibility and take ownership of your education. Don't be afraid to take risks and learn from your mistakes.
- » Master and refine your ability to schedule, manage your time, and organize.
- » Develop your writing skills.
- » Build relationships with your teachers. Attend office hours whenever possible.

With practice, you will find that developing the kind of straight-A study skills outlined in this book really does work. Best of luck in school and beyond!

—Cindy Clumeck Muchnick and Justin Ross Muchnick

# LIVE LIFE
## IN THE
# CLASSROOM

Most adults wake up each morning, get dressed, grab breakfast or coffee, and race out the door to work so they can provide for their families. You have a job, too: school. Your job is to be the best student you can be. And it isn't always easy. Here's how you can do your job really well.

Just like a "regular" employee:

» Show up on time
» Work hard to impress the boss (i.e., the teacher)
» Be nice and pleasant
» Be a team player
» Demonstrate leadership
» Get involved in your community

How do people get promoted and attain positive job recognition from bosses? They work hard by committing to doing the best job possible. Building relationships with your boss and coworkers (in this case, your teachers and fellow students) makes your job easier and allows you to find success in a larger community of workers and leaders.

# WORK WITH TEACHERS YOU MAY NOT LIKE

It's easy to complain about teachers. Maybe you feel a particular teacher doesn't like you. Maybe you have the super-hard teacher who never gives As. Maybe you have the teacher who didn't like your older sibling, so now this instructor has a negative preconception of who you are. Or maybe you have the cranky old teacher who makes you memorize and regurgitate everything she says and then never tests you on it. Well, just as you might not like everyone in the workplace (or even in life, for that matter), you may not like all of your teachers. But, even if you don't like them or their subject, you still have to try hard to do your best. In school, just as in real life, you sometimes have to bite the bullet and perform the way your boss wants you to perform, even if it is uncomfortable. If you treat school as your job, you will be more successful as a student, which will translate to more success in the real world.

# PLEASE THE BOSSES

Your job in school is to work as hard as you can and perform to the best of your ability for your bosses. Here's where it gets tricky. Unlike most employees, who probably report to one boss or supervisor, you have six to eight bosses to please—all of your various teachers. And here's the even trickier part. You have to figure out *what* each one wants, *how* each wants it, *when* each wants it, and then give the assignment to each teacher exactly *that* way. That's what you have to do—even if the assignment isn't fun, even if the subject is not your favorite, and even if you don't respect the teacher.

For example, your English teacher may base a large percentage of your grade on class participation. If so, come prepared and be sure your voice is heard at least a few times a week in his class. Your history teacher may say that he wants to hear your *original* thoughts regarding the lecture or reading assignment. If so, have some ideas ready to share in class, or at minimum, be able to think on your feet during a lecture so you can ask a question or voice a comment. Yes, it is tricky to get to know exactly what each teacher wants from you, but the syllabus, combined with the teacher's first day of class presentation, will give you many clues on how to succeed.

If you can discover each teacher's expectations clearly—and each will be different—your success will be greater. Figuring out what each teacher wants can actually be a fun and challenging task. Does your teacher always check homework? Do it *every* time. Does he speak or pay closer attention to the kids who sit in the front rows? Choose to sit in the front or request to have your assigned seat moved there. Does your teacher frequently mention her office hours? Schedule a meeting and go. Does your teacher encourage outside correspondence via e-mail? Be sure to communicate your questions in that manner.

# WHERE TO SIT

Sit in one of the first three rows of every class. In class, proximity to your teacher is crucial. The boss is up front, looking out and teaching to a classroom full of faces. The faces often blur together from class to class, especially if your teacher teaches multiple courses to multiple grades. Sit up close so you can be certain to be recognized and appreciated as an individual. While it may seem to you that your teachers know you very well, remember that you are one of at least 100 or several hundred students they instruct throughout the day. Be sure they really do know you. Sitting up close just makes that process easier for them.

Studies show that from the vantage point of the front of a classroom or audience, a speaker's eyes scan the room in the form of a reverse capital letter "T." That means the front row(s) and everyone down the middle receives the most eye contact from the teacher. Those sitting on the edge of the room, along the wall aisles, or in the back rows tend to get overlooked. So, if you cannot find a way to get up front, be sure you are sitting in the middle of the classroom.

# CHANGE YOUR SEAT

If you are lucky enough to be in a classroom that has desks arranged in a circle or chairs around one large table or Harkness table (where the teacher sits at a round table with you), then guess what? *Everyone* has a front-row seat, which means you are fortunate to be in a class that easily allows for dialogue, participation, and group interaction. A circular arrangement also prevents you from hiding from your teacher; you have to be actively engaged and alert.

What if you're assigned a seat alphabetically and your last name starts with "Z," so you're assigned to the back row in certain classes? Simply come up with a reason to request that you sit closer forward. How about:

» "I am having trouble hearing from the back row. Can I please move my seat closer up? I don't mind sitting in the aisle along the wall."
» "I'm having trouble seeing the board from the back." If you have glasses or contacts that is a bonus!
» "Are you willing to shift seats when the next term begins? I'd like to sit up closer to feel more connected to what is going on."
» "Is it okay if I found someone in the front who doesn't mind switching seats so I can sit closer to the front?"
» "I focus better in class when I sit farther forward. Is there any way I can move up to get closer to the front rows?"

## CLASSROOM POSTURE

Use good posture in class. For example, be sure to sit up straight. Slumping in your chair or putting your feet up against the chair in front of you can make you sleepy and less alert. Poor posture also sends a message to your teacher that you are disengaged from the presentation. On the other hand, good posture shows your teachers that you are making a conscious effort to learn, and teachers generally take note of that.

The way you sit can also affect your ability to pay attention. If you slouch in the chair, your eyes won't be focused on the speaker. Each time you want to look at the teacher, you will have to lift up your entire head, and the effort needed can disrupt your note taking. Instead, it is much more effective to sit up straight with your back against the chair or seat back. Place the paper in the center of the desk or table and hold it in place with whichever hand you do not use to write. If you sit in this position, you should be able to watch the professor while writing; you also will be able to glance down at your notes by just moving your eyes, not your entire head.

## LEARN FROM CLASSMATES

Think of your classmates as coworkers and the upperclassmen as advisors. Learn which classmates are strong students or class leaders—you might want to consider partnering with them on group projects. You can learn a great deal from your peers and model yourself after them if they have already demonstrated success in a class, gained a strong academic reputation, or appear to be on good terms with the teacher. Try to set up study groups or partners in the subjects that don't come easily to you. If you work with classmates, your brain will be more engaged. How so? Communicating material to others uses many parts of your brain and stimulates you to learn and make connections more than if you study by yourself.

Friends, older siblings, and upperclassmen can be your best resources in school for many reasons. Since they have "been there," many upperclassmen can give you the lowdown on teachers and what is expected of you in class. Seek advice and ask questions of those ahead of you. Older students feel proud to be asked their opinions by younger students. In the realm of confusing teenage social dynamics, that recognition matters. Don't be shy. Be aware that asking five students will yield five different answers, and your solution or answer is probably in pieces of those answers.

# FUEL YOUR BODY

Just as cars need gas and tune-ups to run properly, students need sufficient nourishment and a healthy body to succeed in class. Eat a well-balanced breakfast that includes protein and fresh fruit and get a good night's sleep (eight or more hours). Both food and sleep make a big difference in your alertness, attention span, and absorption of academic material. Athletes are very conscious about what they eat so that they can play their sport to their highest potential. Just like athletic activity exercises your muscles, academic study exercises your brain; therefore, your brain needs to be well nourished to work at its potential.

On another note, bring a water bottle to class in case you get thirsty—this simple tip will save you from leaving class to get a drink, and a sip of water can act as a helpful pick-me-up if you are feeling fatigued or sluggish. You don't want to miss an important lecture point because you're headed to the water fountain. But be sure not to drink *too* much, or you may waste your precious class time in the bathroom!

# DO YOUR HOMEWORK

The most basic rule to being successful in any class is to do your homework. Homework serves as the basic foundation of what you need to do to succeed in your job as a student. It represents the *minimum* expected of you, so be sure you *always* do it. Homework also lets you and your teacher know areas you need to work on and better understand.

Assignments to be done outside of class often comprise a percentage of your grade; do not underestimate the importance of always completing them. Never view them as a waste of time. In addition, homework is meant to assist you in understanding the course material. Doing it can be your best study guide for the tests! And, don't forget, if you don't turn in an assignment or you miss a day of school and don't take the initiative to make up the work, you risk receiving a zero in the grade book. Those zeros add up and average into your final grade. A score of zero or a missed assignment can even go so far as to ruin your grade. In addition, if you don't do homework from the get-go, it will be harder to manage your coursework. You don't want to fall behind.

# MAKE GOOD IMPRESSIONS

The first time you meet teachers or professors, be sure to impress them. If there is time after class (if not, try office hours), introduce yourself to your teacher so she can put a face with a name. In the future, if you need to e-mail or meet with her again you can remind her you were the student who introduced yourself or asked a certain question during class. Don't introduce yourself to teachers just as they arrive at the room or right before class, as usually they are trying to get everyone settled down and organize their materials. The end of class is a more relaxed and natural time, assuming the teacher is not running off to another class. Here are some other suggestions on how you can make a good first impression.

» Arrive on time with the assigned textbooks.
» Sit close to the front of the room.
» Be attentive—no cell phones, doodling, or staring out the window.
» Be engaged in class and have your voice heard when appropriate.
» Take notes, listen well, and maintain eye contact as much as possible.
» Dress tastefully to make a good first impression.
» Ask a question or make a comment to have your voice heard the first day or week of class.
» Say hello to your teacher outside of class.
» Attend the first office hours offered (or the first few) even if you don't need any help. Just go and make some casual conversation or bring a factoid, question, or tidbit to get on your teacher's radar.
» Thank your teacher at the end of class. (You can do it in private if you feel embarrassed in front of other students!)

# BUILD TEACHER RELATIONSHIPS

Teachers serve as great sounding boards to recommend what class you should take next. They often know what their colleagues' classes are like and what class you should place into next year or term (generally, but not always, the next in the sequence). Obviously, the better you have gotten to know your teacher through the course of your term, the more comfortable you will be asking him for his thoughts on what to take next. Also, if you want to continue to an honors, Advanced Placement, or seminar level of a class, you may need both a strong grade in the preliminary class *and* a recommendation from your previous teacher. So, be sure they know who you are!

Additionally, at the conclusion of each class, think about how the strength of your relationship with your teacher could help you in your next academic endeavor. Every teacher is a potential recommender for a summer program, college application, or graduate program. Teachers are willing to write recommendations for hard-working students (regardless of their grades). However, your teachers want to know you before they write about you, so the more substantial your relationship, the more insightful the recommendation will be. Also, studies show that having poor or nonexistent connections with teachers is a primary reason students drop out of school. That's another good reason to build those relationships whenever possible!

## BE YOUR OWN BOSS

Sometimes, you may feel that you have very little choice when it comes to classes, teachers, or your school career; however, everything you do is your choice. *You* are in charge of your job. The school experience can really be summed up as a series of your choices.

» You choose when you want to study or not (even if your parents nag you!).

» You choose whether to play video games or spend the extra time memorizing your Spanish vocabulary words for tomorrow's test.

» You choose whether to text and instant message your friends until all hours of the night or to review those flash cards one last time and get some sleep so you are fresh for a quiz in the morning.

When you think about things that way, you can see how you have more control over your school experience than you first thought.

When faced with these alternatives, remember to choose wisely. The choices you make *do* count. College admission officers take note of everything you have done with your time, inside *and* outside of school, beginning the summer after eighth grade (when you technically are a high school student and primary school graduate). So, it *all counts*. And it is all your choice. The better your choices, the more options you will have later when it comes to colleges. Will you make mistakes? Absolutely. Often times, those mistakes not only make for the greatest learning experiences, but they also serve as terrific nuggets for college essays when it comes time to fill out your applications.

# STUDY THE SYLLABUS

The teacher will give you some obvious clues on how to succeed in her class. The first is the syllabus. That's just a fancy way of describing a handout usually given out on the first day of class, posted online, or both. It is an outline or template of what you can expect for the semester or year. Read and study it closely and be sure you understand what is required of you to succeed in this class. Sometimes, a syllabus is distributed on the first day of class with additional verbal instructions from the teacher, so listen closely. You may learn information from your teacher beyond what is written in the syllabus.

A syllabus usually includes the following:

» **Class Information:** Teacher name, contact information, office hours, office and course location and number, and other pertinent course information.
» **Course Description:** Sometimes taken from a course catalog or prepared by the teacher to summarize the content and scope of what will be taught during the term.
» **Course Objectives:** What the teacher hopes you will gain from this class and goals the teacher has set for students.
» **Texts and Supplies:** A listing of the textbooks or online materials required for the class as well as any special supplies you will need to complete the course (such as a scientific calculator, three-section divided spiral notebook, or compass).
» **Grading Structure:** Typically, percentages of the class and how much each will be weighted among attendance, homework, essays, quizzes, tests, final exam, and participation.
» **Classroom Rules:** Such as no cell phones, whether laptops are allowed, etc.

# TAKE ADVANTAGE OF
# EXTRA CREDIT

Who says nothing in life is free? The best-kept secret in school is extra credit. When offered an opportunity for extra credit, take it! Extra-credit points boost your final grade so they are very important. Any time a teacher offers extra credit, she is seeking answers to a few of these questions: *Who can figure out this extra-tough problem? Who is willing to go beyond the call of duty and do a bit more work on top of what is assigned? Who wants to build up a safety net, just in case he doesn't do as well as he wants on a paper or final exam? Who wants to put a few extra points in the GPA bank?* What's wrong with being the student who is the answer to any of those questions or assumptions? Nothing.

Think of extra credit as free money. It's out there for you to take and keep. And here's the greatest secret of all. If you do the extra credit and get it wrong, even if you miss every part of the assignment, you are no worse off than before you attempted it. In fact, you are even a bit *better* off in the eyes of your teacher, since he sees that you are putting extra effort into the class even if what is being asked is stumping you. Teachers *like* students who put in effort, and when it comes time to hand out grades at the end of the term, they *do* glance at that grade book and see if you have been doing the extra credit, regardless of whether you earned all of the points offered. Just *doing* it does help you. Stay on top of what you need to do and build up that extra cushion for yourself through extra-credit points.

As a side note, many schools allow up to 3 percent increase—from a B+ to an A– for example—for earned extra credit. Those points can certainly add up when your grade is on the cusp.

# REDUCE STRESS

Being stressed can impact your attitude and schoolwork. When homework piles up, presentations are fast approaching, or final exams are just around the corner, students have a tendency to stress out. But remember that worrying actually makes you *less* productive. In situations like these, you sometimes just have to accept the fact that you have a lot of work, put your nose to the grindstone, and finish your homework, prepare your presentation, or study for exams. In addition, make sure to practice some form of stress reduction each day to "turn off your brain" and give it a break from stress and academic thoughts. Yoga, breathing exercises, jogging, or just going for a walk in the fresh air can calm your mind and body when you feel tense. Several colleges have a tradition of a "primal scream" session at midnight during finals week. This community yell lets off steam and makes students realize that they're not alone. If your school doesn't have this tradition, feel free to start it—either as a community or by yourself! As a mellower but equally satisfying alternative, consider a bowl of ice cream or another sweet treat as a stress-reducer.

# WHAT TO BRING TO CLASS

Other than the obvious (book bag, pencil, pen, highlighter, sticky notes, homework, books for the class, etc.), you'll also want a couple of other classroom supplies.

» Bring an assignment book or calendar to organize homework and project due dates, test and quiz dates, and long-term assignment deadlines.

» Bring several pens. Pencils may seem like a good idea for note taking because you can erase and edit with them, but they break and wear down, leaving you to sharpen (or click or twist them) and deal with eraser shavings in class. Pencil is also harder on your eyes than ink due to the paper glare.

» Classrooms or lecture halls can be too hot or too cold depending on the season and the number of people in the room; therefore, it is always a good idea to dress in layers so you can adjust your own temperature as necessary.

» A mini book light (inexpensive and available at all bookstores) can also be helpful to have on hand in courses where the room is darkened for slides or projected images, such as art history or film classes.

Other than bringing physical items, do not forget to bring your positive attitude and mindset—one that is taking in information, questioning, and being thoughtful about the subject matter. Regardless of how much you like or dislike a class or teacher, adopt the attitude that each class offers a new challenge to overcome or topic to investigate and examine, and you can sharpen listening and note-taking skills each day. Come to class prepared, and don't become one of those annoying students who borrow a pen and paper from someone different each week. Have a notebook or binder dedicated to each class, and always bring it with you.

# AVOID DISTRACTIONS
# AND PITFALLS

Avoid distracting people—including yourself—at all costs. Try not to sit next to the cute guy you have a crush on, or your best friend, or anyone with whom you may be tempted to talk, socialize, or flirt. Some students are noisy in the classroom; fidgeting is part of their nature. Gum chewers, frequent texters, or even those with laptops can distract you from your job of being a successful student. Be aware of those classmates and avoid sitting near them.

Turn off your cell phone—not just to vibrate but to off altogether. Double- and triple-check that you have turned it off. Teachers have been known to kick students out of class or throw phones in the trashcan if a ringer or buzzing noise interrupts class. Put all other tempting electronics away, deep in your school bag or locker. Wear a watch so you don't have to turn to look at a classroom wall clock. This may not seem like a big deal, but a teacher can misinterpret your curiosity about the time as boredom or disrespect. Instead of blurting out questions when they pop into your head, jot down possible questions to ask in the margins of your notes and ask when the time is appropriate. Use your pen or pencil to take note of interesting observations or connections you have made during a lecture or reading that you can bring up in class if there is an opportunity.

# PROS AND CONS OF LAPTOPS

Many students and even teachers have begun to bring laptop computers to class. Some find this idea to work well, while others don't like it.

**The Pros:**

» Most people type more quickly than they write by hand.

» You have easy access to the school web page or portal, where applicable.

» Many teachers now e-mail or "dropbox" lessons or handouts during class, making the computer a helpful tool.

**The Cons:**

» Typing on a laptop can distract your fellow students and, worse, your instructor.

» Writing by hand gives you greater flexibility. You can also draw signs, and use arrows and symbols more easily by hand.

» With the Internet you get added distractions. If you are easily distracted, you do not want to have the world wide web at your fingertips during class time.

# SMART BOARDS AND SOCIAL NETWORKS

Though it is your choice whether you bring your own electronic devices into the classroom, be sure to use your teacher's electronic learning aids like SMART Board (if your teacher is fortunate enough to have one) or PowerPoint presentations (if they are given). Perhaps your teacher is media-savvy and uses interactive technology in his presentations.

Many teachers use Skype to communicate and teleconference with classrooms across the world or even incorporate streaming video from YouTube into their lectures. In fact, some schools use educational sites like *www.teachertube.com* to view videos from teachers and students worldwide. Math teachers have started to incorporate websites like *www.hotmath.com* or *www.wolframalpha.com* to introduce new concepts. Video images or music can assist a teacher in illustrating something in a lesson. Some teachers have begun to find benefits in social networks such as Facebook, where they can create closed groups to interact and share information with their students. Other teachers post blogs or conduct podcasts for their students.

Generally, you will find that these interactive doses of modern technology can provide a different and interesting style of learning. The bottom line: Take full advantage of whatever technology your teacher offers to enhance his lesson.

# LEAVE THE RECORDER AT HOME

Some students think they'll take the easy way out by bringing a hand-held recording device to class and rely on that instead of taking notes. However, the recorder ultimately means much more work than you may realize. You will get home and have all that recorded information to review, which means, in effect, going to class twice.

By taking notes in class instead, you're already beginning to digest and edit the information. For example, you might not write down information that you already know or have taken notes on before. You also don't need to write down the detailed explanations your professor makes to recall and understand a particular concept. Since your notes are brief, they will take far less time to read over than it would take to listen to a recorded lecture again.

With a recorder, there's also the problem of technical difficulties. What if the batteries run out or the teacher's voice is too low or muffled? What if you accidentally delete your recording? Minimize these risks by leaving the recorder at home. That said, there is one way that electronic recording may help you. If you must miss a lecture for some reason, ask a friend to record it so you'll be able to keep up. (Be sure this request is okay with the teacher first.) Make sure, though, that as you listen to the lecture you take notes just as if you were sitting in class.

## LISTEN, DON'T JUST HEAR

Have you ever been in the midst of a conversation with someone, nodding your head in agreement, and suddenly found yourself unable to respond to a question he just asked? While you may have technically heard him, you weren't *listening* to him. How about when someone tells you his name and within moments you have forgotten it? Why is listening so difficult?

One reason is that students and adults confuse *hearing* with *listening*. Hearing is *passive*; some sound has been picked up by your ear, whether or not you wanted it to, and there's been a noise. Listening, on the other hand, is an *active* process. It means that you must *do* something to accomplish it. It takes action and, often, work to listen well. For example, let's say you are sitting in a crowded cafeteria talking with a friend. You hear the noise of the cafeteria, the chatter of students around you, the sounds of someone's iPod, and somewhere in all that, you even hear your friend. But to understand what your friend is telling you, you need to *do* something—you need to listen to distinguish her words from all the background noise.

# USE EFFECTIVE LISTENING STRATEGIES

Work hard to listen to the professor's words. Make the effort. Concentrate. It may be difficult at first, but, with practice, you'll get better. Also, pay attention to the speaker. It is difficult to listen to someone if you are not giving all your attention to that person. Ideally, you should look at the speaker's face the entire time she is talking. In a lecture, though, this is not always possible, because you also need to look up and down at your notes from time to time. Try, if you can, to write while keeping your eye on the professor. Your notes may look messier but, in time, you'll get more adept at writing without looking at the page.

If you can't write and look at the professor at the same time, make sure to look up from your notes frequently. This will ensure that you are maintaining a direct line of communication with the teacher. If the professor is explaining a difficult concept, you could be better off not writing and simply looking her. This way, you can actively concentrate on listening and understanding. After the professor is finished, jot down a few notes or phrases to help you remember what was said. Listening, like any skill, improves as you work at it. As you try to concentrate in different situations, you'll find you get better and better. Practice always helps.

## SEE CLEARLY

Have your eyes checked annually. Reading books up close, gluing your eyes to a computer monitor for hours at a time, or squinting at a white board can strain and affect your eyesight. Find out if reading glasses or resting your eyes periodically can help reduce eyestrain. Keep rewetting or lubricating drops on hand just in case your eyes dry out.

## WATCH FOR LAPSES AND CLUES

Become more aware of the times when your mind is drifting to other subjects or your eyes are wandering out the window. When this happens, take a deep breath and focus your attention back on the speaker. Try stretching discreetly, or open your mouth to breathe instead of breathing through your nose. Or, sip some water from your water bottle to wake you up a little bit. Everyone is prone to lapses in attention, and if you can recognize when your mind wanders, you will begin to correct yourself much faster and not miss as much.

Listening effectively means paying attention to more than the speaker's words. People convey a great deal of information through the way they speak as well as what they say. Get in the habit of concentrating on additional signals from a speaker besides spoken words. Take note of the speaker's tone of voice, the volume of his speech, pauses, hand gestures, and body language—these signals can enhance your understanding of the speaker's words. Additionally, by being alert to these elements and spoken words, you have more to occupy your attention, ensuring that you remain actively engaged in the lecture, conversation, or discussion.

# PARTICIPATE IN CLASS

When class participation is part of the grade, many students make the mistake of thinking that they just need to talk a lot to get high marks. However, there are many kinds of comments and questions, and some are much more intelligent and impressive than others. Asking questions indicates your general interest in the class, but students who constantly raise their hands and ask very basic questions about fairly obvious points can make a bad impression—they appear too lazy to make an effort to understand something for themselves or think beyond the basic material. There is, however, a way to phrase a question that sounds more intelligent. For example, if you simply raise your hand and say, "I really don't get this. What does it all mean?" you sound like you just don't want to make the effort to understand the topic. On the other hand, if you say to a professor, "I see the point about Y and Z, but I'm having trouble understanding how they relate to X," you are asking a more specific question that reflects work to try and understand something. Try to make your questions as specific as possible to indicate you have some knowledge and a genuine interest in clarifying a point.

## AVOID PIGGYBACKING; SEEK ALTERNATIVES

Another way students earn credit for class participation is by making comments during class discussions. Some students who feel compelled to say something in class will blurt out whatever pops into their heads. If the comments restate something that has already been said or merely points out something obvious, it won't impress the teacher; in fact, it can indicate the students haven't been paying close attention. This type of remark is known as a "piggyback" answer, one that just hops onto something someone else said and does not demonstrate your originality. If you want to make a general comment, make sure it contributes something meaningful or makes a new point.

Not everyone is comfortable participating in class discussions or asking questions in front of large groups. If you are one of those people, consider letting the teacher know outside of class that it is a challenge for you to speak in class, but also work on overcoming this fear or impediment since it is a life skill that will be important in future classes and in the workplace. Perhaps smaller class discussion sections will be a better place for you to have your voice heard. Look into taking a public speaking class, which might provide you with some confidence and tools to assist you in speaking in front of an audience. Not speaking up doesn't necessarily detract from the class participation portion of a grade. If you are shy or uncomfortable with offering comments in class, be sure to visit the professor during office hours and discuss the course—this will demonstrate that you have an active interest in the class and subject matter.

# CHAPTER 1

# SUMMARY

» Build relationships with your teachers and classmates.
» Treat school as your job and you will be more successful as a student, which will translate to more success in the real world.
» Discover each teacher's expectations clearly.
» Sit in one of the first three rows of every class.
» Request a change of seat if you are not able to sit close to the teacher.
» Use good posture in class.
» Learn from your classmates, not just from your teachers.
» Food and sleep make a big difference in your alertness, attention span, and absorption of academic material, so eat and sleep well.
» Do your homework always.
» Make a good first impression.
» Build strong teacher relationships.
» Be your own boss. The better your choices, the more options you will have later.
» Read and study the syllabus closely and be sure you understand what is required of you to succeed in class.
» Think of extra credit as free money and attempt to do it always.
» Practice some form of stress reduction each day to "turn off your brain" and give it a break from stress and academic thoughts.
» Have a notebook or binder dedicated to each class, and always bring it with you.
» Avoid distracting people while in class.

- » Review the pros and cons of laptop use in class and decide what works for you.
- » Take full advantage of whatever technology your teacher offers to enhance his lesson.
- » Practice good listening skills and strategies. Don't just hear, listen.
- » Participate in class discussions, but don't piggyback.

# CHOOSE COURSES CAREFULLY

Think of choosing your classes as shopping for clothes. You can try things on for size and then determine what is the best fit. Selecting your classes can be based on a variety of factors including teacher reputation, class reputation, your ability level in that subject, and sometimes, just what fits into your schedule. The first two weeks of any term, school year, or semester is affectionately known by many students as "the shopping period." With shiny new school supplies and sharpened pencils in hand, fresh-faced students venture out to class, ready to dive into new subject matter, explore new teachers and material, or continue with and explore more deeply the subject matter that they enjoy.

Before you select classes, do some preliminary research. First and foremost, think about whether the subject matter is interesting to you. Read the course description and find out if there is a sample syllabus available to look at—ask at the department office or go online to look. Check out the reading list to see if it looks interesting. You can even go to the bookstore to look over the books themselves. To find out about a particular professor, ask around and talk to fellow students. Don't assume that just because a professor is famous or has won awards, he is a good teacher; schools sometimes hire big-name professors for their academic reputations, not for their teaching abilities. You might even try sitting in on a professor's class to see what he is like. Finally, don't feel concerned about dropping a college class two weeks in; drops don't mean you're a quitter. Remember, you're focusing on choosing a class that's the right fit for you.

# HIGH SCHOOL VERSUS COLLEGE SHOPPING

In high school, a school college counselor or guidance counselor can help you find classes that are appropriate. If you're a freshman or sophomore in high school, you may not have much choice in the classes you can take. You're usually limited to choosing a class that is in either the regular college prep track, honors, or Advanced Placement (AP). Other than that, most courses in high school are simply basic requirements that need to be met. As you move into your junior and senior year, however, you may be able to choose some electives that match your interests. For example, you may get to pick which foreign language or science class to take to fulfill the graduation requirement. High school guidance counselors may know which courses are offered during each particular class period, so if you end up dropping a class, ask them to help you fill that time slot. Sometimes a class is just not the right fit.

If you're in high school, talk to your guidance counselor about how to tackle the class (perhaps by seeing a tutor to catch up), or change it if possible (to find a class more suited to you). If you're in college, consider dropping the class and finding another.

# WHEN TO CHOOSE CHALLENGING CLASSES

Choose your classes wisely and carefully, both in high school and college. Straight As in honors and AP classes mean something different than straight As in a regular college preparatory track with no advanced coursework. How can a college distinguish between its applicants from so many varied high schools? First understand this idea: Colleges evaluate you by how you perform within the context of your school and what is offered there. That's why you should consider signing up to take the hardest classes you are capable of surviving. Choose the most difficult classes you can take in the areas that come easiest to you and in which you naturally excel. If you love history and have done well in prior history classes, an AP history class might be a good choice. But if you usually struggle at math, there's no sense in trying to tackle an advanced calculus class.

A good rule of thumb is: If you think there is a chance you will get a C in the honors or AP class, take the regular level class. If you can pull an A or B, you should be stretching yourself to take honors or advanced level courses. If you think it's a better idea to try to get straight As in regular track classes in order to "look good" for college, think again!

Don't take the easy way out by just coasting through high school in regular track. Colleges will see right through that. Do the best job you can and aim high by challenging yourself as much as you can. In college, the same is true. Once you've narrowed down your field of study, go ahead and take the most challenging classes you can handle. Once you've graduated and are working, you'll be glad that you learned as much as you could in college. And, if you think you *may* plan to continue on and apply to graduate school, you want to show that you've challenged yourself in your coursework. Just like in high school, you want to show that you didn't take the easy way to a diploma.

## LAZINESS AND THE EASY WAY OUT

Mark Twain once wrote, "Don't let school get in the way of your education." What he meant was that traditional classroom- and book-learning are not how all of your education takes place. There are many experiences beyond the four walls of your classroom that shape and educate you in different ways as well. Travel experiences, late-night talks in your dorm room, online learning, leadership and camp experiences, school clubs and organizations, and athletics are just a few other venues and experiences where you can learn.

Skipping class, sleeping late, relying on purchased lecture notes, or reading CliffsNotes instead of doing your job of being a student always comes back to bite you in the form of bad grades or a bad reputation among your teachers and classmates. School is certainly full of temptations, distractions, and a multitude of activities to juggle simultaneously. If you opt just to coast through school by doing the bare minimum, you will be missing out on a great deal of learning and many academic opportunities, and, at some point, your bad habits will come back to haunt you. By the time this happens, it may be too late to dig yourself out of the hole you have created. Bad grades can lead to summer school, community college as your only option after high school, retaking a course, or Ds and Fs on your permanent transcript or academic record.

# WHEN TO TAKE A BREAK

When schoolwork becomes such a chore that you find you're taking shortcuts and cheating yourself out of a deeper learning experience, then it may be time to take a personal pause. If you need a breather from school, seek the guidance of your teacher, counselor, or parents. Sometimes, taking a break to refocus or have a nontraditional educational experience such as studying abroad or getting a job is just the motivation you need to recharge your battery until you are ready to return and complete school. If you are thinking of this option, have a solid plan in place for what you'll do on your "break" (hint: it must be something constructive!) and how long it will last.

What if you don't feel ready to attend college? Students bloom at different times in their academic careers. For some, high school is a piece of cake, but for others it is a painful struggle. Community college is a good alternative when you recognize you need to get yourself together and demonstrate to admissions that you have figured out how to be a good student.

# CLASS SELECTION AND TRANSCRIPT ANALYSIS

------------------------------

Your transcript is a very important document that reflects all your courses and grades in school. College and graduate school admission officers will all agree that the number one factor in making admission or rejection decisions is the transcript—the courses you take and the grades you earn as a student in your school. Yes, many other factors are considered when you apply to college or graduate school (e.g., your standardized test scores, extracurricular involvement, jobs, volunteer experiences, summer experiences, internships, honors and awards, teacher recommendations, counselor report, personal statement, and other supplemental college essays). But, by and large, *the transcript demonstrates to admission officers your selections and achievements in those academic disciplines and serves as the strongest indicator of the kind of student you are within the context of your own school.* Information about your academic performance is valuable in predicting how successful you will be at the next level.

# WHAT DO COLLEGES AND GRADUATE PROGRAMS REVIEW?

------------------------------

1. The **degree of difficulty** of the coursework you take within the context of your school is assessed by colleges. Colleges receive an academic profile from each high school listing all of the

courses offered at every one of more than 40,000 high schools in America. This profile shows all of the classes available at the individual school, including college prep courses, honors/accelerated classes, and AP offerings. An admission officer evaluates each candidate based on the grades earned as well as the degree of difficulty in the student's course load.

2. Your **grade patterns** are direct comparisons between first and second semester grades earned. Admission directors like to see students with grade patterns that improve—or at minimum, stay the same—from one semester to the next. If you earned a B in the first semester, you can impress admission officers if you earned a B+, or better yet, some form of an A in the second semester. (If the class is only a one-semester class, you should work even harder to do well, since there is only one shot to succeed.) That improvement demonstrates you have mastery of the subject or have grown to absorb the material over time as the content gets more difficult or in depth. On the other hand, a student whose grades tend to go down in the second semester sends a different message. Perhaps the student could not master the harder material in the more difficult second semester. Or perhaps the student began to "tune out" as summertime drew closer. A grade dip can never imply good things. All of your grades dropping in one particular semester will also send up red flags. Be prepared to justify the dip with an explanation to colleges (hopefully a legitimate one—mono or another long-term illness, a loss or divorce in your family, etc.) as opposed to just saying, "Summer-itis kicked in second semester!"

3. **Grade Trends** are the year-to-year movement of your grades. Did your grades improve as you advanced each year or did they worsen? How did you do overall from freshman through junior year or high school or college? Did your grades make an upward turn as you matured or did things spiral downward over the course of each year? Again, the closer you get to higher-level work (i.e., junior year and the fall of senior year), the closer you are in the eyes of admission officers to being a potential student on their campus. The stakes keep getting higher. Expectations increase about your ability, level of responsibility, learning process, and approach to courses. If you're worried about your own grade trends, don't be afraid to seek help.

4. **Additional academic experiences** demonstrate whether you went beyond what was offered in your school. Did you seek out additional academic experiences (such as community college, summer programs, independent study, or research)? High school students worry if their school does not offer AP or honors classes. Will you be penalized in the eyes of admission officers? Not if you explore other options! Here are some ideas of things you can do to supplement and enhance your transcript:

- Take an online class in a course that your school does not offer or at a more advanced level than offered by your school.
- Seek out courses at a local community college. Most of the time, courses are transferable to your high school, and in some cases, the grade you earn can even be added to your high school transcript.
- Approach a teacher in a class you enjoy(ed) and see if you could be a Teacher's Aide (TA) or if the teacher will do an independent study with you.

# SAVE YOUR OLD PAPERS

Clearly, course selection can impact your academic career later, so consider saving some of your old graded papers, writing, tests, research papers, or projects. Why? Here's one reason. Some programs will ask for a writing sample or example of good work you did in high school or college. If you have saved some of your best work, complete with positive teacher comments, this request will be easy for you.

Many students dump work at the end of the school year, only to realize later that they may have been better off keeping some of it. Even a graded math test that shows your work and thought process can be insightful to admission officers! A paper you reprint off your computer is of less value than a graded one with teacher comments. So save those papers with grades and teacher comments in case you are asked to provide photocopied or scanned samples later.

# CHAPTER 2
# SUMMARY

» Choose a class that's the right fit for you.

» Choose the most difficult classes you can take in the areas that come easiest to you and in which you more naturally excel.

» Don't choose to coast through school by doing the bare minimum. You will not only be missing out on a great number of learning and academic opportunities, but at some point your bad habits will come back to haunt you.

» If you need a breather from school, seek the guidance of your teacher, counselor, or parents.

» Your transcript is a very important document that reflects all your courses and grades in school. Know what high schools and colleges are looking for.

» Save papers with grades and teacher comments in case you are asked to provide photocopied or scanned samples later.

------------

# BUILD TEACHER RELATIONSHIPS

Teachers have lives outside of school. They don't just live at school to serve their students (although most are extremely passionate about what they do). At the end of each day of work, teachers go home, do laundry, take showers, talk on the phone, watch TV, surf the Internet, exercise, and eat dinner. Whether it seems like it or not, teachers are people, too, and are ultimately there to educate, support, and help you. Don't forget that even though teachers are doing their jobs, they *do* have a life outside of school. So it is very important, in fact *essential* if you want to succeed, that you show respect for your teachers.

# KISSING UP IS OKAY

Don't worry if your classmates call you a "kiss up." While you don't want to become unlikeable in their estimation, take a step back and realize that your reputation in school does not live with you forever; if you really network, you will be well liked by both your fellow students and your teachers. If you see your teacher outside of class in the hallway, parking lot, at the grocery store, or wherever else, what should you do? Look him in the eye, say hello, and show respect.

The importance of teacher relationships can't be stressed enough. You want all your teachers to view you as a good kid. Even if you describe yourself as a shy person, step up to the plate and say hello. Better yet, when you see a teacher, try to think on your feet and make reference to something recent you did in class such as, "Hey, Mrs. Stockstill, that was a hard math test." Or, "Mrs. McCarty, have a great weekend. I'll be cranking out that paper!" Just say something—*anything*—that shows you are treating the adult who happens to be your classroom boss with respect and friendliness. Don't be embarrassed or afraid if your peers are nearby when you make contact with your teachers. Your teachers will appreciate your effort to build a relationship with them—or just to be friendly—outside of class. Being extra-friendly is a good way to build meaningful relationships and get the teachers on your side.

# PRACTICE LIFE SKILLS
# WITH TEACHERS

Talking with your teachers is a great way to practice your interacting-with-adults skills. You will need these skills when you try to find a job, work with a community-service coordinator, plan classes with your advisor or college counselor, or even interact with your religious leader. Teachers can also help you try to work out your academic (and sometimes even social) concerns. They will make useful suggestions to help you improve, and teachers appreciate students who come to them to seek help. Don't be afraid or intimidated, no matter what your classmates may say about a teacher. Teachers select this profession because they genuinely *want* to educate and connect with teens.

Here are some sample phrases to say to your teacher if you see one of them outside of class:

» **Good:** "Hey, Mrs. Robinson."
» **Generic but fine:** "Hi, Mrs. Ratnesar. Have a great weekend."
» **Better:** "Hey, Mr. Peters, that bonus question was a toughie on the test today."
» **Even better is a reference to current class work:** "Mr. Gapp, I'll be working on my problem sets tonight!" (or some other comment relating to the work you are doing for his class).
» **The million-dollar-quick-thinking-on-your-feet comment:** "Mrs. Johnson, did you see the presidential debate last night on the news? It was set up in a similar format to the parliamentary debate style that we learned about in class!" (This is a stellar way to make some connection from what you learned in class to the outside world. Teachers *love* this type of comment because it helps them know that you are really grasping what they're teaching.)

# TAKE PRIDE IN YOUR WORK

Being a conscientious student means you take pride in your work; it indicates you are not just going through the motions of showing up for class but are taking your work seriously. In turn, this shows that you respect your teacher and the lessons that he is trying to teach you. The quality of the work you turn in also indicates how conscientious you are. For example, an essay that has been carefully proofread and neatly printed shows you've put work into it and care about how it appears. An essay rife with spelling or grammatical errors and smudged with last night's dinner, your morning coffee, or pencil marks sends the message that you really don't care that much about the work. That, in turn, says to your teacher that you don't respect his class. While there are specific things to do that show how conscientious you are, you also need to adopt a committed attitude.

If you take pride in your work as a student and approach your job seriously, everything you do will reflect this positive attitude. A committed attitude shows your teacher that you're willing to learn and will help them overlook a poor quiz grade here and there.

# BE ACCOUNTABLE FOR MISTAKES

What happens if you bomb a test? Receive a poor grade on an essay you wrote? Feel totally confused and frustrated in a particular class? Go to your teacher first. Be proactive and try to get help from your teacher before you involve your parents. Why? *Because it is time for you to take charge of your academic experience.* Don't be the student whose parents call the teacher every time he gets a grade that disappoints. Teachers hate this (and if you're over eighteen, they can't talk to your parents without your permission anyway). Conversely, don't be the student whose teacher has to call his parents because he's not taking his work seriously.

If you don't feel comfortable approaching your teacher about the problem, *then* it's time to talk to your parents. They may be able to help you strategize about what to say, or role-play the interaction between you and your teacher. Of course, if you encounter any sort of harassment or inappropriate behavior on the part of your teacher, do not try to handle it yourself. Immediately involve your parents or a school authority. Teachers respect students who stand up for themselves in a polite way, even if the students don't agree with them.

Be respectful and careful with your words, but do stand up for yourself when necessary. For example, if you disagree with an essay grade, ask the teacher nicely to help you understand why you got that grade. Ask what you could have done to earn a higher grade. Explain thoughtfully and specifically why you think your work was better than the grade indicates. Even if the grade doesn't change, you've shown the teacher that you care about your work.

# TEACHERS ARE SMART

Some students think they can easily outsmart the teacher. Keep in mind, though, that your teacher was once a student too. Any tricks you think of, your teacher has probably already experienced. Consider this popular story passed on from one student to another about an incident that supposedly took place at an American college.

As the story goes, four college buddies decided to take a weekend ski trip, even though they had a major exam coming up Monday afternoon. They had a great weekend partying, but on their way home Monday morning, they realized none of them had studied. They decided to skip the exam and make up an excuse. When they went to class the following Wednesday, they told the professor they had been driving to class Monday morning from their off-campus apartment, when they'd gotten a flat tire several miles away from school. They tried to fix it as fast as they could, they said, but the flat detained them for several hours and forced them to miss the exam. The professor expressed sympathy for their plight and told them they could make up the exam that Friday. The four friends were thrilled that they got all this extra time to study. They showed up at the classroom Friday completely prepared for the exam. The professor passed out the test and when the four friends turned over the exam, they were horrified to find this one question: "Which tire on your car had the flat?"

The moral of this story: Don't lie to your teacher. Respect the time she puts into preparing for the class and be accountable for your behavior.

# FIND A MENTOR

Your friends, family, and upperclassmen can offer you advice on many things, but a teacher is perhaps the best qualified to offer specific advice about your education. For that reason, finding a faculty member who can serve as your mentor is extremely important. In addition to offering you advice, a mentor can help you negotiate the school's bureaucracy, discuss your future career or educational plans, write letters of recommendation, and much more. Finding a mentor takes time and effort. There's no sign-up sheet, and no professor is going to knock on your door to volunteer. You need to find a teacher whom you like and respect, and then work to establish a relationship. At some point, you will take a course with a teacher whom you really admire. You can initially see this person during office hours or after class. On the first couple of visits, simply discuss the course. If the professor seems receptive, you can eventually ask for advice on other aspects of your education and volunteer more information about your own interests and goals.

## MAINTAIN MENTOR RELATIONSHIPS

Seek out a mentor who can assist you in networking with colleagues or partners they know in the working world or who can offer you an internship. Mentors do not have to be teachers. They can also be coaches, employers, school administrators, graduate students, or residential advisors. If you meet with the teacher or professor several times during the semester, you should begin to feel you are establishing a relationship. The key to finding a professor who becomes your mentor, though, is to maintain that relationship once the class is over. Don't let a solid relationship with a teacher slip away. Make certain you continue meeting with the teacher, even if you are no longer taking her class. This won't be too difficult to do if she has become involved in helping you plan your future in some way. An extra adult sounding board outside of your own parents is always a helpful addition to the support network you build for yourself.

# MAKE A GOOD IMPRESSION

There's no way around the fact that grades are a central part of measuring success at most schools. A large portion of a grade is based on objective information, such as the number of short-answer questions you got right or wrong or the number of days you attended class. A small part of your grade, however, is subjective—it is based in large part on the teacher's impression of you. While this impression can't change the number of exam responses you got right or wrong, it can influence other aspects of your final grade. For example, a final grade will often reflect a grade for class participation or effort, which is much more difficult to quantify than the number of right or wrong responses. It is extremely important that you try to make a good impression.

You also need to be careful how you do it. If you overdo your effort, it can seem insincere and backfire. For example, if you interrupt the lecture or class discussion simply to make some comment that you think demonstrates how smart you are, you will not impress the teacher. Moreover, she might resent that you've interrupted class for an unrelated point in an obvious attempt to gain favor. The impression you want to convey is not necessarily how smart you are, but that you are a conscientious student who is willing to work hard to learn. Having a great attendance record and visiting the teacher outside of class can help make this impression.

# HAVE A PERFECT ATTENDANCE RECORD

Nothing is more off-putting to a teacher than a student who consistently arrives late to class, or even worse, one who doesn't attend at all. Coming late disrupts the entire class and, more unfortunately, indicates to the teacher that you don't care about her class. Even in a large lecture course where you think you might slip in unnoticed, a teacher can spot you coming in late. Therefore, make it a habit to get to class on time. If you have a special reason for being late, make certain you see the professor during office hours to explain the situation and apologize. Even better, tell the professor ahead of time so she has a heads-up.

Coming late to class is a disruption; not coming at all is a major problem that can seriously affect your grade. In some smaller classes, a teacher will take attendance. If this is the case, you should make sure that you go as often as possible. Having perfect attendance will probably impress the teacher when it comes time to grade you on class participation. Even if a teacher does not take attendance, it is still worth going to class all the time. For one thing, being there on a regular basis ensures that you are exposed to all the course material, which in itself will probably improve your grade. Moreover, if you attend class regularly, the teacher will recognize you as a familiar face.

# MAKING THE MOST OF OFFICE VISITS

------------------------------------

While a teacher will usually know you by name in a small class or seminar, it is almost impossible for her to know you personally in a large lecture class. You should, therefore, make sure to see the professor at least once during office hours to introduce yourself.

There are many reasons why teachers hold office hours. First, teachers want to offer a time to be accessible to their students outside of class in order to foster a more personal dialogue and provide attention to students. Also, office hours provide students opportunities to discuss problems, concerns, or questions they have about the subject matter.

When you do visit your teacher's office, be prepared with your questions and comments so that he does not feel you are wasting his time. To help break the ice, try to come up with a specific question to ask about the class or about a particular lecture. During the course of your discussion, you can tell the professor a bit about yourself and your academic interests and aspirations. Doing this ensures that the teacher has an impression of you as an individual, not as another face in the crowd. Here are some suggestions of what to say or do when you see the instructor for office hours:

» Review essays you have written and seek additional guidance based on the comments.
» Bring in tests or quizzes with answers you got wrong and ask to review them.
» Prepare a comment you have considered or debate a point the teacher made (as long as you substantiate it) to demonstrate that you have

thought about what you learned in class and applied it to the world outside of class.

» Bring in any other questions from class notes, handouts, or readings that may have confused you. Don't be shy about visiting your teachers outside of class time and building an independent rapport with them.

# TEACHER RECOMMENDATIONS

Building good teacher relationships will pay off tenfold when it comes time to ask for a recommendation for a summer program, college, graduate program, or job. Teacher recommendations are testimonies about your performance and contributions in class that educators provide for your colleges, graduate schools, or future employers. The comments in these recommendations are taken very seriously and serve as an important piece of selection criteria. Sometimes they are the only way evaluators can get a real sense of who you are as a student, which in turn offers them an indication of your potential as a college or graduate student or future employee. The better a teacher knows you and the more support and advance notice they have in writing your recommendations, the better.

How can you obtain terrific, personal recommendations?  Build good relationships with your teachers by sitting close to the front in their classes, doing extra credit assignments, frequenting office hours, being friendly whenever you see them outside of class, and so on. When you ask your teacher to write you a recommendation, provide him with a copy of your student resume or "brag sheet," which lists your extracurricular

activities, community service, awards, honors, jobs, hobbies, and interests. Give your teacher plenty of time to write these recommendations
by giving him the forms or online links well in advance of the deadline.
Provide a sample of graded work from the class with comments, if applicable. Jot down some bullet points of ways you have contributed to his
class (this is sometimes called a "student blurb"). After the teacher turns
in your letter, don't forget to write a thank-you note and let him know
where you were admitted and how his letter helped.

# BUILD YOUR BRAG SHEET

A brag sheet is basically an extracurricular resume. It is a place for you
to list everything you have done outside of the classroom—after school,
on the weekends, and during summer. List all honors, awards, accomplishments, extracurricular activities, summer experiences, internships,
employment, community service, and athletics in which you have participated or achieved, as well as hobbies and interests that you have.
Include a column listing the hours per week and weeks per year dedicated to each activity. Keep this growing log in a document on your
computer and track your involvement since the summer after eighth
grade. Don't forget about any awards or honors you have won in these
activities! If you begin keeping a log in the summer after eighth grade,
you will be ready to list your activities on college applications by senior
year. When writing a brag sheet or any resume, list your jobs or history
in reverse chronological order (the most recent to the furthest back in

time). Also, list items in terms of most hours committed to least hours committed to demonstrate which activities required more of your time.

# WRITE A STUDENT BLURB

A student blurb is a short, bulleted list of your individual accomplishments and reflections on your contribution in a particular class. In it, you can list some highlights of your recollections of the course along with any real examples of how you added to the classroom experience through a particular debate, conversation, or question. The more specific examples you can recall about your performance in the class, the better. You will give your student blurb to your teacher along with your brag sheet (as discussed previously) so she can use the information to help formulate a recommendation. If you are lucky, your teacher may sprinkle in some of the actual tidbits you wrote about yourself into the recommendation! Teachers have dozens of these letters to write a year and they are time-consuming; the more assistance, support, and lead time you can give to them to aid in the process, the better.

**Sample Student Blurb:**
*Literature*
*Justin Muchnick, Class of 2012*
*Eighth Grade, Teacher: Mrs. Duke*
*First Semester Grade: 97%*
*Second Semester Grade: 96%*

- » Acted out trial scene of *To Kill a Mockingbird* and played role of Atticus Finch.
- » Every essay I wrote achieved distinction on the "Wall of Fame."
- » Wrote final essay on Harper Lee and her viewpoints on racism and made connections to the 1950s and 1960s civil rights movement.
- » Presented interactive video project about Act V of *Macbeth*.
- » Active in class discussions about the *Narrative of the Life of Frederick Douglass*.
- » Participated in debate on slavery and its role in the Civil War.
- » Led conversation on *Animal Farm* and its parallels to pre- and postwar Russia.

# WRITE A THANK-YOU NOTE

Always thank a teacher for taking time to write you a recommendation. Teachers are not paid any extra money to spend time writing thoughtfully about you. A proper thank-you note, possibly along with a small gift, is a gesture that is always appreciated. Make sure your thank-you is not e-mailed or left in a voicemail, but handwritten, the old-fashioned way. Below is a simple example you can follow and modify for your purposes.

*Dear Mr. Rogers,*

*Thank you again for taking time out of your busy schedule to write me a letter of recommendation for Andover. I realize that this is extra work for you and just wanted to thank you for your willingness to write on my behalf. I have thoroughly enjoyed being your student. [Add a few more* personal sentences about you or the teacher, for example:] *I love how you go beyond the lesson plan to teach in an interdisciplinary way. For example, the lectures you gave on Robert Kennedy's 1968 speech in Indianapolis really inspired me to learn more about this great political figure. I also enjoyed your references to* Waiting for Godot, *which introduced me to Theater of the Absurd. I will truly look back on my year in your literature class as one of the most interesting and thought-provoking academic experiences I have had. You have set the bar high for all of my future teachers; you really are a hard act to follow.*

*Best regards,*

*Justin Muchnick*

# CHAPTER 3

# SUMMARY

» Teachers are people, too, and are ultimately there to educate, support, and help you.

» Teachers appreciate your effort to build a relationship with them—or just to be friendly—outside of class.

» Talking with your teachers is a great way to practice your interacting-with-adults skills.

» Take pride in your work; it indicates you are not just going through the motions of showing up for class, but are taking your work seriously.

» Be accountable for mistakes and go to your teacher first before involving your parents or an advisor.

» Teachers are smart. Any tricks you think of, your teacher has probably already experienced.

» Find a faculty member who can serve as your mentor and maintain that relationship.

» Make a good impression. A small part of your grade is subjective—it is based in large part on the teacher's impression of you.

» Make it a habit to get to class on time. Try to have a perfect attendance record.

» Attend office hours at least once per term.

» Building good teacher relationships will pay off greatly when it comes time to ask for a recommendation for a summer program, college, graduate program, or job.

» Build a brag sheet and make a student blurb.

» Write your teacher a thank-you note after they write you a recommendation.

# MANAGE TIME EFFICIENTLY

## TIME FLIES

While "management" seems to be a term often used for those with careers and adults in the business world, remember that you have a job, too: being a student. To do this job well, you need to gain some of your very own managerial skills. You are your own manager; therefore, you must allocate and break down your time into useful, practical, worthwhile chunks for studying, class time, socializing, extracurricular activities, sleep, exercise, meals, and more. Time is precious and does fly, so divide it up accordingly, and use it wisely. There are twenty-four hours in a day, approximately eight of which you use to sleep, eight of which you use to attend your school or job, and eight for every other task in your life including doing homework, joining extracurricular activities, socializing, tending to family obligations, working, eating, doing laundry, going to the gym, going to the grocery store, etc. How you choose to spend your time can make or break your academic career.

# TIME MANAGEMENT PLAN

Managing your time takes a plan and heightened awareness of what tasks need to be accomplished in a certain amount of time. Meeting deadlines in an organized manner allows you to enjoy not only the result of your efforts, but also the journey and hard work it takes to achieve results. Here are a few time management exercises you can try:

» Count how many hours you spend on the main activities in your life: school, transportation, work, athletics, extracurricular activities, socializing, eating, sleeping, studying, etc., and compare your list against the 168 hours there are in a week. This will give you an idea of how much of a handle you have on your time. This exercise can be a real wake-up call if you never seem to know how you ran out of time to get everything done.

» Don't spend more time anticipating and worrying than acting. Instead, take active steps in planning out your time and begin to take action. Nike's famous motto, "Just do it," has become a significant statement in our culture for a reason.

» Spend time organizing e-mails and electronic files into a filing system and delete what you don't need. Just as you throw away junk mail you receive through snail mail, don't be afraid to delete items in your e-mail inbox. File away content that you may need access to later in an orderly manner. The same goes for paper files. Dump what you don't need and organize what you do need into your filing system. Taking the extra moment to follow an organization system will save you hours of frustration later.

Pencil in a schedule by half- or quarter-hour blocks for times when you are slated for something (class, appointment, workout, practice, etc.) and you can see where you have holes or gaps of time to fill with anything that needs to be done.

## MORE TIME MANAGEMENT TIPS

Remember, there is often "dead time" built into your school day. Sometimes free periods or a break between classes can serve as "found time." Instead of socializing or procrastinating, use those free periods as a time to get ahead on your work. Wear a watch or carry a device that easily tells you the time. If you want, set your watch five minutes fast. It can help keep you on time. Also, invest in a small egg timer, which you can purchase at your local grocery store. If you need to be reminded of your increments of study time or your schedule, a timer's bell will alert you. Old-fashioned timers are easier than programming cell phones or PDA devices to keep you in check.

## CREATE A TO-DO LIST

Whether you jot your action items on a piece of scrap paper or keep it on your cell phone, maintain a running list of things to do. Though you may think that you are able to remember everything without writing it down, something will slip through the cracks. Write down your list!

Another benefit to writing down your list is that you can cross off or delete items from it. You can enjoy a sense of accomplishment in completing a task, no matter how mundane, and it means one less thing to worry about. However, that crossed-off item probably will be replaced quickly by something else. Think of your to-do list as an endless load of laundry. Once you finish washing, drying, and folding, there are always more dirty clothes piling up! Keep your list with you at all times for reference. If you are extra-organized, consider prioritizing your list in order of importance or grouping tasks into categories based on where you need to accomplish them (i.e., things located geographically near each other) or by theme (such as homework, sports, personal).

## EFFECTIVE SCHEDULING

Many study guides instruct you to set a rigid schedule for yourself in which each minute of each day is devoted to fulfilling a certain task. These schedules block off time for everything from study sessions to mealtimes to hours when you can 'sleep. But here's the problem: schedules like these are virtually impossible to follow. What if, for example, you don't feel like eating dinner at exactly 6:30 on a particular night? What if you are supposed to study from 8:00 to 11:00 on Tuesdays, but one week your professor wants you to attend a guest lecture at the same time? What if there is a really good party on a Friday night you want to attend, but you don't have time scheduled for it? What do you do?

Have *some* kind of schedule so that you can keep track of what needs to be done and leave yourself enough time to do it. Instead of making a rigid schedule, you can plan a more general one that will allow you to make changes on a week-to-week and day-to-day basis. This general schedule only shows those activities you do every week of the semester at the exact same time. You should make it up at the beginning of the semester, before classes have actually started. Make a chart listing days of the week at the top, and the hours of the day in a column on the left side. You can choose to make your schedule through a computerized program such as iCal or Yahoo! Calendar, but be sure you have a portable version with you accessible through your phone or iPad. Alternately, print out a few weeks of calendar at a time, which you can carry around in your backpack, adjust, write on, and refer to as necessary.

# MAKE A FLEXIBLE SCHEDULE

Student life is far too chaotic to be squeezed into a neat, orderly schedule. Your schedule will change frequently: one week you may have a major exam or a paper due that will require more work; another week, you may have to devote substantial time to an extracurricular activity. Even study tasks, such as reading lecture notes or assigned texts, will take different amounts of time each week. One week, the assigned readings may be very difficult and take twelve hours to complete, while another week, the readings will be substantially easier and only take four hours. But if you are stuck in a rigid schedule, you won't be able to make the necessary adjustments to provide the time you need. So how do you make a flexible schedule?

First, find out the meeting times of all your classes, and block off those times on the schedule. Then, mark off any times that will be consistently unavailable to study—for example, when a club or a team meets. As shifts occur in scheduling, such as added review sessions or study groups, be sure to note them promptly in your calendar as well. After you've blocked off those hours, you'll be able to see the times each day that are free. Those free times can be spent any number of ways (studying, doing work, socializing with friends, etc.). You can decide each week exactly how you can best use those free times.

## WEEKLY LISTS

During the week, work on each task that needs to be done during the time you've designated for it. Don't force yourself to spend an exact amount of time on each task since these are estimates. Take each task as it comes—some will take more time than you anticipate; some will take less. Just make sure that by the end of the week you've fulfilled all the tasks you set for yourself.

In addition to making a weekly list of specific tasks, it's a good idea to make a to-do list for each day. Before you go to sleep each night, you can quickly make a list of the things you need to accomplish the following day. You can include, in addition to study tasks, any specific errands you need to run—from doing laundry to returning books to the library.

That way, you've got all your tasks in one place and you won't forget to do something. As you do each one, cross it off the list so you can see yourself making progress and take pride in your accomplishment.

# SET PRIORITIES IN YOUR SCHEDULE

Some weeks, you will have an especially heavy workload and face a severe time crunch. To establish a priority to your tasks, look at your list for the week and try to rank your tasks in order of importance. For example, completing an assignment that will soon be due or studying for an upcoming major exam will take priority over most other activities. Decide not only what is due at your first deadline but also what may take you the longest to finish or the assignment or task that you find the most difficult. Expend your energy when you are the freshest (e.g., at the beginning of your study time or early in the morning) on work that is more challenging for you. After identifying what is most important for that week, be certain you devote most of your time to fulfilling those tasks. If you finish them, spend the remaining time on the less important ones. If you don't get to the less important tasks, you can make up for it in later weeks when your workload is lighter. Just be certain you catch up at some point so you don't fall too far behind.

# FREE PERIODS AND FREE TIME

It is called a free period since, technically, it is a block of time that you have free to do what you please. Don't let the word "free" fool you, though. Even though you are "given" this time to do what you want, you need to think about maximizing all your free or found time to address your weakest academic areas.

» Can you use a free period to do some extra studying and review for an upcoming test?
» Can you use the time to attend office hours for a teacher whom you never are free to meet due to scheduling conflicts?
» Can you encourage classmates to share study tips and quiz one another during your common free periods?

Absolutely yes to all of these.

Sometimes a class gets cancelled at the last minute because there is no substitute teacher prepared to teach the missed lesson. Bingo! You have just received the gift of free time to use at your discretion. On the other hand, everyone needs time away from work, but you shouldn't "schedule in" these times. As a student, your priority is fulfilling your study requirements, as well as commitments to extracurricular activities. These will take up a certain portion of time each week. When these tasks are complete, any time that remains is yours to do with as you please. This free time is healthy and beneficial for you to find balance in your life. Your job as a student should not be all-consuming, or you risk burning out or missing out on many other aspects of student life such as socializing, joining organizations, playing a sport, volunteering, eating, and sleeping.

# SET GOALS

As you get bogged down in the day-to-day life of being a student, you may find yourself daydreaming about what you'll do after school. Instead of letting those daydreams rob you of free time, channel that energy into reminding yourself why you're working so hard in the first place. Set both "big-picture" and smaller goals.

To determine a big-picture goal, consider your purpose in attending school. If the only reason is because your parents (or the government) said you must, you are not going to be very happy. There must be *something* you hope to gain in your studies, and it doesn't necessarily have to be the same thing your parents or teachers want you to gain. You may, for example, want to develop specific skills to help you in a certain career. Or, you might want to receive high grades so you can get into the college or graduate school of your choice. There might be more personal factors involved as well, such as the desire to better yourself, to become a more educated person, or to experience new ways of thinking and seeing.

Your big-picture is a personal goal, and it can be different from everyone else's. Keep this big picture in mind as you study and navigate school. Without a sense of this big picture, you can easily feel unfocused; however, if you maintain a clear sense of what you are doing and why you are doing it, you are more likely to remain on track. Try to see how each task on your to-do list and schedule fits into your big-picture goal. If you see how each agenda item contributes something to your goals, you'll remain much more focused on your work (and you'll also find your studies more fulfilling).

Goals don't have to be simply big picture, though. For each to-do list item, you should set a short-term goal, such as reading a chapter of a textbook thoroughly or studying for an upcoming exam. At the same time, though, you should set larger goals for your entire education and understand that all of the short-term goals help you get closer to the big one.

# AVOID EXTRACURRICULAR OVERLOAD

If you find that your after-school activities are taking up too much of your time, pick one after-school practice, rehearsal, or meeting to skip each week. If you are an athlete with a large time commitment of multiple practices per week, consider telling your coach that your parents are now requiring you to work with a tutor weekly to improve your grades. If you are in college, you could simply say that you need extra academic help. Coaches may be upset with this request, but they will generally comply because most high school and college athletic teams require that you maintain a minimum grade point average. By asking this of your coaches, you can buy yourself two to three more hours of free time per week.

It's important to remember that although extracurricular activities are a great addition to your academic life, they are just an "extra" (hence *extra*curricular). Your main job is to be a good student. Offer yourself the best opportunity for academic success. Found time can relieve much pressure, and you sometimes need to find it by eliminating something from an already-overbooked calendar. If a large chunk of your extracurricular time is spent doing any activity other than a sport (such as a school club, theater, musical instrument, etc.), you can also make the same request to your activity leader. Tell her that you need to miss one of the weekly meetings in order to get some tutoring to improve your grades. Eliminating one weekly commitment will surely help you recover some "lost" time.

# AVOID PROCRASTINATION

"I'll save it for later," "I'll get to it eventually," "Maybe next time." If you find yourself increasingly relying on these excuses, it means you are suffering symptoms of procrastination. Who wants to do schoolwork, study for a test, or write a paper when the sun is shining and the beach is beckoning? Perhaps the newest video game was just released and you just *have* to try it out, or the newest blockbuster film is in the theaters. What makes you procrastinate? Temptations are all around you. They include:

» Your computer—often the very tool you need to complete an assignment—loaded with games, distracting music, and, of course, the Internet!
» Your friends who text, call, IM, Skype, or visit and want to hang out instead of studying.

- » Your TV, iPod, cell phone, or other electronic gadget that is much more fun to interact with than a boring homework assignment or vocabulary flashcards.
- » Restaurants, the refrigerator, coffee shops, shopping malls, or your car.

You're not going to want to study every time you are supposed to. Nevertheless, you're going to have to motivate yourself somehow to do work even when you don't feel like it.

# USE A REWARD SYSTEM

Avoid procrastination by setting up a system of rewards as motivation. For example, after you've completed your study tasks for a particular day, give yourself the time left as your personal free time. This in itself serves as a reward to get you motivated to work. For example, if you know you want to watch television at night, you can force yourself to work efficiently during the day. Similarly, if you want to go skiing one weekend, you'll try your hardest to get all your work done during the week. You just need to remind yourself of the fun activities waiting for you when you are finished working.

Sometimes, even with the promise of free time as a reward, you may still find it difficult to get motivated and begin working. If that's the case, provide yourself with additional rewards as you study. Set small goals, and reward yourself each time you fulfill them. For example, if you have several hours blocked off on Tuesday night for reading 100 pages, promise yourself a snack after you've gotten halfway through the

assignment. This will, at least, get you started. Work in smaller increments, such as twenty minutes at a time, and then stretch, drink a
beverage, eat some M&M's, or respond to an e-mail. Then go back to
work for another twenty minutes. Depending on the subject, the increments may be longer or more bearable. These rewards don't need to
be extravagant. A reward can simply be a short break to do something
you like—getting ice cream, talking on the phone, going for a walk, listening to music, or whatever else. When you finish a major task, such
as completing an essay or taking a final exam, it's nice to give yourself
a bigger reward—download some new songs or have a fun night out.
These rewards will help you get through the more difficult work periods
of the school year.

# CHAPTER 4

# SUMMARY

» Break down and allocate your time into useful, practical, worthwhile chunks for studying, class time, socializing, extracurricular activities, sleep, exercise, meals, and more. Divide your time up accordingly, and spend it wisely.

» Try some time management exercises to help you accomplish all of your tasks.

» Maintain a running list of things to do and a schedule of your time commitments.

» Prioritize your tasks. Look at your list for the week and try to rank your tasks in order of importance.

» Budget your time and take advantage of free periods.

» Set "big-picture" and "small-picture" goals.

» If your after-school activities are taking up too much of your time, pick one after-school practice, rehearsal, or meeting to skip each week.

» Don't procrastinate. Avoid procrastinating by setting up a system of rewards as motivation.

--- --- --- --- --- ---

# TAKE GOOD NOTES

While it is important to be a good listener and participant in class, you also need to master the art of taking good notes so that you can refer back to them later. Some find the note-taking process to be tedious while others find it effortless. Finding a system that works for you is an important task that will make the rest of your student life easier.

When your workload increases and the material becomes more sophisticated, your notes must reflect that growth in your learning. So much of what you learn, and retain comes from attending class and becoming a competent note taker. Many teachers and professors offer information in their lectures that goes above and beyond what's in your textbook or other class materials. And that additional information inevitably ends up on an exam! The good news is, if you approach note taking as a job or a skill you can master, you will build a solid foundation that will help you achieve academic success. The better and more committed you are to devising a strong in-class system of note taking, the better off you will be later, when you need to use your notes to review or complete assignments out of class. This chapter will provide an eight-step outline of an effective strategy for taking notes in class:

1. Arrive on time.
2. Make preparations.
3. Identify the key terms.
4. Write down all key terms.
5. Define and explain the key terms.
6. Develop your own shorthand.
7. Construct a rough outline.
8. Note the general themes of the lecture.

# 1. ARRIVE ON TIME

That's right, the first step is pretty easy! Even better than arriving on time: arrive a few minutes early if you can. It's difficult to take effective notes on the first few minutes of the lecture if you rush to class, arriving out of breath and flustered. By coming early, you can relax and decompress for a few minutes and put yourself in the right frame of mind. If you have time, you should review your notes from the previous class to help focus your attention on the day's subject matter. Besides helping you get settled, arriving on time is just common courtesy. Dashing in late can distract and offend the teacher, and it's never a good idea to upset the professor.

# 2. MAKE PREPARATIONS

When you get to class, take out a new sheet of paper or flip to a new page in your notebook. You should always start each class with a fresh piece of paper because lectures tend to have their own separate topics or themes. By keeping separate notes, you can better identify distinct themes.

Make sure to have the right writing instrument to take great notes. Select a decent ballpoint pen or a sharpened pencil for taking notes in class and have an extra available. Always put the date and subject at the top of the first sheet, so you can put them in the proper binder or file at home. While spiral-bound notebooks may seem the easiest, most efficient, and lightest weight option for your book bag, instead consider using plain, single-sheet, loose-leaf paper and binders instead. Loose-leaf paper (the kind with three holes that you can put in and take out of a binder notebook) works best because you won't have to bring your entire binder to class. It also enables you to add additional notes, rewrite notes, or shift pages without difficulty, and to file everything away after the semester is over. One thin binder for each class will allow you to move pages of notes around as you add to or modify what you do in class. It also allows you to insert handouts you received from your teacher next to your notes about that particular subject.

# 3. IDENTIFY THE KEY TERMS

During lectures, teachers mainly communicate new information. Some of it is specific, such as names of people or places, significant dates, or certain theories, formulas, and concepts. These are the *key terms* of the lecture. Most often, these terms are going to be new to you, making them harder to remember. The goal of note taking, then, is to keep track of all these expressions. Your teacher may even write down items on the board for the class. You should *always* note anything a teacher writes on the board. But there will also be many other terms that an instructor might not write—if these are new to you, write them down as well. If you write down just these key terms, you'll have a pretty accurate representation of the entire lecture. These terms are most often the highlights and key points around which the entire lecture is based. You can be certain that if you showed your professor this list of terms, she would be able to recreate the lecture for you in its entirety.

As you listen to the lecture for key terms, listen for other signals your teacher gives you that highlight important points that she wants you to know. Phrases such as, "The most important _____," "Three key points about _____," or "This will be on the test," indicate the speaker is presenting something worth writing down and reviewing later. Also, throughout any lecture, listen for specific phrases and terms, such as, "to sum up," "in conclusion," "especially," and "therefore," that indicate a professor is emphasizing a major point.

# 4. WRITE DOWN ALL KEY TERMS

You are not going to be able to write down everything the teacher says, and you should not try! If you attempt to write down everything, you'll find yourself in deep trouble. At some point, no matter how fast you can write, you will miss something. Either you won't hear clearly, or you'll become distracted, or your hand will cramp up. And then, if you're like many students, you'll panic. As you struggle to figure out what you missed, you'll miss even more. And, before you know it, you won't have notes for the majority of the lecture. Let's make it clear right from the beginning. *You don't have to write down everything.* Your next question probably is, "So what exactly am I supposed to write down?" In order to answer that question, you need to examine the purpose of taking notes. In taking notes, your aim should *not* be to create an exact transcript of the professor's lecture. If that were the case, the professor would simply hand out photocopies. A great deal of what you hear in class might be familiar to you and, therefore, doesn't really need to be recorded. Your priority should be to write down information and concepts that are new or unfamiliar.

# 5. DEFINE AND EXPLAIN
# THE KEY TERMS

Write brief explanations or definitions of the key terms next to them, whenever possible. Again, don't write down everything the professor says. Try to jot down just a few words or phrases that will help you remember what a term means. If you can't write much about a particular term, don't worry. *Just keep listening and writing!* You'll have plenty of time to fill in more information later. If your professor has moved on to introduce a new topic or key term while you are still taking notes on a previous one, then leave that term behind. Keeping up with required reading can help when you take notes, as you will already feel somewhat familiar with the material. Key terms from reading assignments are often reinforced in class and vice versa. You don't need to write perfect, grammatically correct sentences. These notes are written only for you; as long as they make sense to you, nothing else really matters.

# 6. DEVELOP YOUR OWN
# SHORTHAND

Shorthand is a method for writing quickly using symbols or shortened versions of words. Try to develop your own kind of shorthand; this will enable you to write down more material faster and with less effort. Many study guides teach formulas and codes for taking notes in shorthand. The problem with these methods is that you wind up having notes that are practically written in secret code! Don't make your notes overly complicated by developing all kinds of crazy signs and formulas. Find a way to take notes that make sense to you. Some basic ways to develop a shorthand that is simple and easy to read are to:

» Avoid complete sentences.
» Keep descriptions, examples, and anecdotes brief.
» Abbreviate only *repeated* key terms.
» Use signs and symbols.
» Sketch charts and diagrams.

Don't take notes with different-colored pens or highlighters. Taking notes in different colors can be time-consuming and distracting. While attending class, you should remain focused on the teacher, not on color-coding your notes.

# 7. CONSTRUCT A ROUGH OUTLINE

The key terms we've been discussing don't exist in isolation. They are part of a larger structure that is the professor's lecture. Each term ties in to some bigger topic or point being addressed. As you write down those key terms, you can begin to construct a rough outline in your notes that will help you see how larger topics and various terms are related. Think of the lecture as a puzzle. Later on, after stepping back from your assignment, you can see how it relates to what else was presented in your class. This way, you can make a more detailed outline outside of class.

# 8. NOTE THE GENERAL THEMES OF THE LECTURE

In most cases, a lecture focuses on a main topic. At the start of the class, you should already have a general idea what this is. Teachers who hand out a syllabus or post one online usually list lecture titles with dates beside each of them. Check your schedule and be sure to see what your instructor has planned for each class. The day's required reading can also give you a sense of what the lecture will address.

Knowing the main topic is an important factor. As you take notes, remember that each new piece of information must somehow fit in. Try to figure out what each new piece has to do with the main topic. Some ideas may be central, while others may be less important. In your outline, indicate those that are more connected to the primary idea. Here are a few tricks to figuring out what the most important points are within any given lecture:

» Note what's repeated.
» Watch body language and listen for tone of voice.
» Focus on the beginnings and endings of a lecture.

# SEMINARS: TAKING NOTES ON DISCUSSIONS

In addition to lectures, many of your classes may be seminars, where students participate in smaller group discussions led by the professor, an upperclassman, or a TA. In addition to your in-class discussions, you can sometimes have an opportunity to discuss something before or after a lecture. When taking notes during seminars or discussions, your concerns are somewhat different from those during lectures. Discussions in seminars are less oriented toward key terms and much less structured. Often, they are an opportunity to review and flesh out ideas that may have been less clear from either the professor or the reading. Here are some suggestions on how to gather the most important information from seminars.

» Listen more, write less, and participate.
» Look for key terms.
» Note topics of discussion.
» Note the professor's opinions.

# SAVE OLD NOTES AND SOME TEXTBOOKS

Many students are so relieved when the semester is over that they throw away all their notes. That type of housekeeping is a serious mistake. You've worked hard taking those notes! And, more important, there might be a time when you need to refer back to them. Be a pack rat. You never know what you will need again. Be assured that many of the courses you take will interconnect, particularly those within your college major or concentration. As you move on to more advanced levels of coursework, you'll find you need to refer to notes from earlier courses to refresh your memory about certain key points or fundamentals. You also may take courses that seem completely unrelated to one another, only to find that some point or issue will come up that you have previously addressed elsewhere. For example, you may be reading a novel in an English class that refers to specific events from your history class. If you've taken a history class about that period, you can read your notes and get more information about those events, which in turn, can help you understand the novel and allow you to contribute more to class discussions. Imagine how impressed your teacher will be if, in a class discussion, you can provide some of that background information. So save your notes!

In addition, consider holding on to some of your textbooks and other course materials. It's tempting at the end of the semester to sell all your books back to the bookstore, especially given how expensive books are these days. However, if there is any chance you will refer to a book—particularly if it was used in a course that is part of your major—it is probably worthwhile to hold on to it. One option is to sell only the textbooks and keep all other books. Textbooks tend to be more expensive than other books, and you get back a significant amount of money. Other books are often resold for only a fraction of the original cost (especially if they are paperbacks).

# CHAPTER 5
# SUMMARY

» Arrive on time. It's difficult to take effective notes on the first few minutes of the lecture if you rush to class, arriving out of breath and flustered.

» Make preparations. Take out a new sheet of paper or flip to a new page in your notebook when you arrive in class.

» Identify the key terms, such as names of people or places, significant dates, or certain theories, formulas, and concepts.

» Write down all key terms. Define and explain the key terms.

» Develop your own shorthand.

» Construct a rough outline.

» Note the general themes of the lecture or seminar.

» Save old notes and some textbooks for reference later.

# WRITE STRONG RESEARCH PAPERS

The essence of writing is communication. Writing essays for a class requires you to communicate things you have learned back to the teacher. Both taking tests and writing essays center on how well you communicate. Many people think writing is all about correct grammar and spelling, but an essay can have flawless grammar and still not say anything. In any work of writing, you are communicating your ideas, thoughts, and beliefs to someone in a way that makes those ideas clearly understandable. When you are immersed in writing an essay, you can easily forget that you are trying to communicate with a specific person—your teacher, who will grade the essay. You should always keep this in mind: *What can you write that will most impress your teacher?*

A teacher is probably not going to be overly impressed by flawless grammar and spelling; she'll expect those features in a good student's work. What will impress the teacher is the quality and strength of your ideas—those are the crucial components of a good essay. They must be communicated in a manner that makes them accessible to the reader.

Coming up with sophisticated and intelligent ideas is your responsibility; no book can give them to you. This chapter teaches you how to communicate those ideas in a way that will show them off. Using a step-by-step approach to writing essays, you'll ensure that your ideas are communicated in a clear, organized, and powerful manner. Finally, don't be afraid to take some risks with your writing. Chances are, your first idea is one that many of your classmates have already had, so strive to be original. Your work will stand out more and demonstrate to your teacher that you have a voice of your own.

## FIND A TOPIC

To a large extent, the topic you choose determines the results of the final product. Obviously, an original and exciting topic will more likely result in an original and exciting essay. Therefore, you should not choose a topic haphazardly. Your choice of topic must take into account the requirements and nature of the assignment. Sometimes a teacher will assign a very specific topic and provide you with detailed requirements that tell you exactly what the essay should address. Yet even with the most rigidly defined assignment, you will have room to maneuver. In this case, the challenge is to view the topic from your own point of view and, somehow, make the subject of the essay your own. You will need to spend time thinking about the assignment and how you plan to approach it in your own individual manner. At other times, a teacher will suggest several topics or provide you with a very loosely defined assignment that gives you a great deal of freedom. Don't make the mistake of thinking that being allowed to choose your own topic makes the essay easier to write. Having free rein with an essay is exciting, but it is also overwhelming. There are so many possibilities for topics; how are you supposed to find one that's right for you? Make the right choice by selecting one that excites or interests you.

# CONSIDER YOUR AUDIENCE

Good writers always direct their work to the proper audience. For example, you would write a letter requesting a job interview with an entirely different tone and word choice than you would write a love letter. In the case of a school essay, your audience will be the teacher who assigned and will grade the paper. Before you begin work, be certain that you understand the assignment, are aware of the teacher's expectations, and know the *exact* requirements for the essay. How much research should you be conducting? How long should the essay be? What format should you use? Are there any specific details you should include or address?

You might also want to choose a topic that your teacher will find unique. Many teachers become bored reading the same topics over and over again; most will, therefore, welcome a paper written on something that is, in their opinion, different or unique. For example, if everyone else in the class is writing about a certain work of literature, consider choosing something else. Just make sure that your teacher is open to new ideas and atypical subjects. It may seem difficult to be original, especially if you are writing about a topic such as an historical event or literary work that has been discussed by others for centuries. The way you approach this topic, though, can add a new twist to it that makes it seem original.

If your teacher gives a prompt, follow it but still try to show some original thought in your work. Don't take a cookie-cutter approach that may look similar to the efforts of all your classmates. Your writing is one of the most direct forms of communication between you and your teacher. What your teacher sees in your writing contributes significantly to the impression she has of you. An essay that is sloppy, unfocused, and filled with typos and grammatical errors paints a portrait of a student who doesn't care that much about what he has submitted. On the other hand, an essay that is neat, well organized, filled with interesting and original ideas, and carefully proofread indicates that the student takes pride in his work. You can guess which student will get a higher grade on the essay (and for class participation). Remember, your essay tells the teacher a lot about both your comprehension and work ethic.

## WHAT INTERESTS YOU?

If you have a more open-ended assignment with a choice of topics, choose one that, first and foremost, interests you. You are going to spend a great deal of time working on this essay, and if the topic itself doesn't pique your curiosity, those hours will seem even longer and the writing process will be even more tedious. If you choose a subject you sincerely want to learn more about, then the process of researching and writing the essay will be interesting and engaging. Think about the various themes and topics that have been addressed in class, as well as the reading assignments you've completed.

» Was there a particular one that you enjoyed learning about?
» Was there anything you only touched on in class that you wanted to know more about?
» Did you have an intense emotional reaction to anything?
» Do you want to express a particular opinion or point of view that you had about one of these topics?

Your writing reflects you; be certain your essay shows you have a serious, professional attitude about your work. Your topic should also be broad enough that you can fill the essay with strong ideas that keep the reader engaged. Of course, you may not be able to settle on a specific topic right at the start. Don't worry! You do not have to! It's fine to begin with a broad, general topic and then gradually narrow it down until you hit upon a more specific theme that satisfies the assignment's requirements.

# LENGTH REQUIREMENTS

An essay is meant to be a detailed, in-depth study of a particular subject. In order to write a solid, focused essay, you should choose a topic that can be addressed fully and comprehensively within the page requirements set by the teacher. If you choose a topic that is too broad for the paper's length requirements, you will end up writing about it in simplistic, superficial terms. You won't have the space to get into much detail, so the entire essay will be written on a broad and obvious level. For example, it would be difficult to write an essay on Robert A. Caro's *The Years of Lyndon Johnson* books in only six pages; you'd have to discuss each of his four massive volumes in one or two pages in order to address them all. If you choose a more limited topic, such as Lyndon Johnson's taking office after John Kennedy's assassination, and address that subject in depth, you will have an easier topic.

You can play around with fonts, margin size, and headers and footers once your essay is done, if your teacher has not already set these requirements (some teachers discuss this in their syllabi). If there is a word-length recommendation, check your word count to be sure you do not exceed or fall short of it by too much. If you do exceed the recommended word limit, try to keep it minimal. On the other hand, don't try to make up for a short essay by padding; your teacher will notice. Students often initially choose topics that are too broad because the students are concerned about meeting the page requirements. At first, six or seven pages sound like a lot to fill up, so you might select an extensive topic to guarantee you have enough to write. Once you begin thinking about and researching your topic in depth, however, you'll often find you have plenty of material. In fact, you may find you need to leave some material out. Yet choosing a topic that is too limited is also a problem. If your topic is too narrow, you may find yourself bending over backwards to meet the page requirements. For example, it would be difficult to find enough original thoughts to express on a single chapter of Caro's *The Passage of Power* in a twenty-five page essay; you would probably run out of ideas after the first few pages and end up reiterating the same points.

# A PLACE TO START

Here are some general topics that would make good starting points for researching an essay:

» A particular work of literature, article or text, or body of work.
» An author, person, or particular group of individuals.
» An historical period or event, or contemporary news event.
» A literary period or genre.
» A scientific field or subfield, in either the general sciences or social sciences.
» A particular issue or subject of debate, either historical or contemporary.

All of the above are broad subjects that would take lengthy papers to examine fully. They all make good *starting* points for selecting an essay topic; you can choose one and begin to think and read more about it. As you do, you'll gradually be able to narrow the subject down to a topic appropriate for the length of your essay.

# READ, THINK, PERCOLATE

After you've chosen a general topic, immerse yourself in the subject matter by reading and thinking about it. By doing this, you can learn more about the subject and generate ideas to use in your essay. You also begin to narrow the general issue down to a more specific one. Start by reading anything you can find that relates to your chosen subject. You can begin with online search engines. You can, for example, consult a general online encyclopedia to see if there is a related entry. Make sure you pick a thorough, academic encyclopedia such as *Encyclopaedia Britannica, Encyclopedia Americana*, or *Collier's Encyclopedia*. You can also find many specialized dictionaries and encyclopedias that address specific fields of study.

Next, using the library's online search program, search the stacks of the library for general books on your topic. Pick books that look promising and copy down their call numbers. Sometimes, all of the books related to that subject will be located in the same section of the library, so you can go to that section and browse. Select a few books that seem interesting and read sections of them. You don't necessarily need to read the entire book. For example, reading the introduction to a book may provide you with a great deal of information.

You can also do a similar type of research at your local bookstore. Grab a notebook or your laptop and spend time in the aisle where your books are grouped. If you are writing an essay that centers on a specific text, such as a particular book or article, it is crucial that you reread that text several times. As you read, jot down any ideas that pop into your head that might make a contribution to an essay. Reading the text a few times may provide you with enough ideas to get started on your essay.

Don't expect yourself to think of ideas right away; your mind needs to let information percolate for a while. Soon, you'll begin making connections with things you've learned, forming your own opinions, and gaining insight into the material. As you continue reading, your ideas and interests will become more focused and defined, and you will be able to narrow down your topic.

# CREATE A THESIS STATEMENT

The key to any essay is its thesis statement. Think of it as the essay's backbone: it is a central idea that holds together the various parts of the essay. The thesis statement is not the same thing as your topic, although they are closely related. Your topic is a general subject that you've thought about to generate specific ideas. By putting together some of these specific ideas, you are able to formulate a particular point of view about some aspect of the topic. This viewpoint, condensed into a single sentence that sums up the central idea of the essay, is your thesis statement. *Every expository essay should have a thesis statement, and all ideas expressed in the paper should reflect it.* Without the thesis statement, the essay is merely a random list of ideas lacking clear, definable points. The essay, in turn, represents the detailed argument that supports this viewpoint. Most teachers prefer this kind of essay; they are interested in your own perspective, rather than a summary of information. The more original the thesis statement, the more original—and impressive—your essay will be.

Once you have an idea of what you want your thesis statement to be, discuss it with your teacher. Clearing the statement with him will assure that you are on the right track. Your teacher may also have suggestions on how to conduct research and organize the essay. You may need to fine-tune your thesis statement. Until you've actually begun writing, it is perfectly acceptable to have only a general sense of your argument. As you conduct research and gain more knowledge, you'll continue to develop your ideas.

# EFFECTIVE THESIS STATEMENTS

In order for a thesis statement to be effective, it should:

» **Be specific.** An effective thesis statement should not be too broad or general; instead, it should say something very specific about your topic. This will ensure that the essay remains focused and does not include unrelated, distracting points.

» **Reflect your own ideas.** Most professors will be more impressed when you express your own thoughts and ideas rather then regurgitating someone else's. Therefore, an effective thesis statement will be original and reflect your own viewpoint on the subject. Make sure that the thesis is phrased entirely *in your own words*.

» **Be something you believe.** The body of the essay must make a convincing argument supporting the thesis statement. It is extremely difficult to present a solid argument supporting an idea that you don't actually believe is true. Moreover, if the thesis statement reflects a personal belief, the entire essay will bear the strength of your convictions. Don't hinder yourself by choosing a thesis statement you don't support.

» **Be something you can build a solid argument to support.** Since your goal in writing an essay is to convince your reader that your thesis statement is accurate, you want to prove your viewpoint beyond a shadow of a doubt. So, be certain you pick a thesis you can prove. When you actually begin conducting research, you may find that you don't necessarily agree with your thesis or that you cannot prove it. If that happens, change the thesis statement.

» **Be a single, direct sentence.** Most academic essays are limited in length; you probably won't have to write a book-length dissertation for every assignment. Therefore, you don't need a long, detailed thesis statement. Be sure you can phrase it in one sentence. If you can't do it in one sentence, it indicates you are unfocused and confused about your idea, or that you've chosen a thesis too ambitious or ambiguous to be proven in a single essay.

# CHOOSE A TITLE

Students often fail to put good titles on their essays. However, the title, which indicates the general topic of your paper, is an important component—it gives the reader a first impression of the writer. Try to craft a title that conveys information about the essay but is also intelligent and witty. One effective strategy is to use a title and subtitle, separated by a colon. The title should be a short phrase or quotation; the subtitle that follows should be a longer phrase or a sentence that explains the essay's topic in more detail. For example:

» *To Kill a Mockingbird:* The Literary Weapon of the Civil Rights Movement
» Dynasties in Different Galaxies: How Caesar and Palpatine Built Their Empires

When writing titles, remember:

» Capitalize the first letters of all words in the title except for articles, prepositions, and conjunctions.
» Capitalize the first letters of the first and last word, even if they are articles, prepositions, or conjunctions.
» Never put the entire title in quotation marks. However, if there is a quoted phrase within the title, you should put that in quotation marks.
» Never italicize the entire title. If you mention the title of a major work within the title, though, you should italicize that.
» Never put a period at the end of a title.

# GET STARTED AND FIND YOUR VOICE

One of the more difficult aspects of crafting an essay is actually beginning to write. Even after all the research, it can be very intimidating to sit down in front of a blank computer screen. Part of the difficulty comes from the way many students tend to view writing. Some students don't think of it as a process and only value the finished product, which their teacher expects to be flawless. This way of approaching it, however, places tremendous pressure on you. If you think your writing needs to be perfect on the first try, you might freeze up with panic, afraid to commit yourself to a single word.

Regardless of whether you need to conduct research, the heart of the essay should always be your own ideas. As you refine your ideas, your own voice and style will emerge. In the course of researching and thinking about your topic, you will develop certain ideas and a sense of the major points you want to make. These ideas will still be in your head, where they are probably mixed together. In order to become a compelling, powerful essay, these ideas need to be organized in a logical manner. You need to get them out on paper, so you can examine them and plan a strategic way to address them.

Your writing should sound like you are speaking to your reader. (Though, obviously the words "um," "like," or other stumbling words do not appear!) Your reader should be comfortable hearing you through your words. Using humor in your writing can also be effective and welcome when appropriate to the context.

## WRITING STYLE

- - - - - - - - - - - - - - - - - - - - - - - -

Every piece of writing has its own style. The style reflects the manner in which something is written, and it depends on such factors as the choice of words, sentence patterns, and the way ideas are introduced. An essay's style indicates the writer's attitude toward the material and signals to the reader how to respond. For example, the style can indicate if a work is serious, sarcastic, humorous, or silly.

Be careful about addressing your reader or the teacher directly in your writing. While your tone can be friendly, actually saying the words "you" or "reader" or asking the reader a direct question is not usually a good idea. When you are writing an academic essay, you generally want to use a serious, intelligent style. Avoid being too chatty or conversational. Avoid using slang or casual expressions; instead, use a sophisticated but realistic vocabulary. Write sentences that are more varied and complex in structure than "See Ross run." At the same time, don't overdo it. If you try too hard to write in an academic manner, the essay might become too confusing and will not sound like your own voice.

Good writing takes time and effort to produce. You can't expect to get the essay right on the first try; in fact, you shouldn't even attempt to. Instead, it's better to write in stages, making changes and improvements with each draft.

## BECOME A GREAT RESEARCHER

Researching for an essay or paper can be a painstaking and tedious process. It can also be very rewarding if you think of yourself as an investigator trying to find clues to help you sort out your assignment. Being a researcher means you seek the ideas of others to confirm or deny your thesis statement or assigned topic. Once you research a project or paper you become part of a much bigger world of academia.

There are essentially two kinds of essays: those that require you to do research from outside sources and those that do not. Essays that include research use information from outside sources to explain and support your thesis. Those that do not focus solely on your own thoughts and ideas about a particular topic. Your teacher will tell you whether you are expected to do research and include other sources in your essay. If the teacher doesn't tell you, ask! Again, think of research as detective work. You are investigating your topic in search of clues that will help you reach a result (your final essay). Using quotes, facts, and other informative nuggets in your writing you clue your reader into your process and investigative expertise.

# PRIMARY AND SECONDARY SOURCES

There are two kinds of sources: *primary* and *secondary*. Primary sources are any texts that are the product of the subject of the essay, such as specific works of literature, historical documents, or essays and articles that present certain theories and philosophies. For example, if you are writing about some of George Orwell's books, then *Animal Farm* and *1984* would be primary sources. If your essay centers on a primary source, you must make certain you read it in detail and take notes on it.

Many essays also incorporate secondary sources. These are books and articles by critics, historians, scholars, and other writers who comment on and address primary sources, as well as other topics and subjects.

If your essay involves conducting research, you need to track down secondary sources that address your topic and take notes on them.

# WHERE TO FIND POSSIBLE SOURCES

There are many sources that address your topic, but, before you can read them, you need to find them. Fortunately, there are several resources you can turn to for help:

**The Online Library Catalog.** Except for very old-fashioned or elementary libraries that still use card catalogs, most libraries now list their holdings on computer. The entries are usually organized in four ways: by author, title, subject, or keywords. If you have a specific source in mind, you can consult either the author or title entries to find out if the library has the material and where it is located. If you are merely looking for general information, though, you can search according to the subject. Most libraries organize their subject catalogs according to the standard list set by the Library of Congress, although some libraries have their own classifications. The library should have a subject list available for you to consult. Sometimes, a topic will be divided into subcategories. Try to find the subcategory that most closely relates to your topic, and use books from that area for your research.

**Published Bibliographies and Indexes.** There are many published bibliographies and indexes that list books and other sources, such as academic journals and periodical articles, on a particular subject. A citation is a listing that includes key information about the book, such as the author, title, publisher, and, often, a brief summary of the source's content.

**The Internet.** Obviously, the Internet is a valuable tool for finding sources. You can access indexes and bibliographies, and also find entire articles from newspapers, magazines, and periodicals. Just be careful of Googling every question you have and relying on Wikipedia for your sources.

Wikipedia is an open site that allows information to be updated and changed easily. Double-check the sources and facts you find there, particularly if the topic you're writing on is the subject of controversy. Since Wikipedia is a database of millions of articles that can be edited by anyone with Internet access, be cautious in your approach to its content. There's nothing wrong with using Google, Yahoo!, Alta Vista, or other search engines as a place to start database searches, but be sure your sources are reliable before citing them in your research.

# THE LIBRARIAN AND THE LIBRARY

Your library has much to offer, so be sure to use it in your quest for academic success. First and foremost, librarians are one of the most vital resources in the library; they can provide you with a tremendous amount of help for just about any academic project you pursue. Ask the librarians questions—that's why they're there. In addition, it's a good idea to wander around your library or take a brief tour to find out exactly what the library offers. Then take advantage of it.

If you use the library properly, its resources can make your job of being a student much, much easier. Become familiar with your library as a source of information, not just as a quiet space where you can study. Finding the perfect quote or the right reference source can be very exciting and empowering as you achieve academic success. Remember, however, when a book is located in the reference section, you will not be allowed to take it out of the library. You'll have to photocopy relevant sections or sit in the library and take notes on the source. The advantage, though, is that you know the books will always be there.

In addition to books, libraries house many other research materials, including magazines, newspapers, journals, videotapes, audiotapes, CDs, and maps. These materials are usually kept in their own rooms or sections. You can ask the librarian or check the library directory to find where these sections are. Magazines, periodicals, and scholarly journals are sometimes bound together in volumes and shelved in the stacks. This is why bibliographies list a volume number in addition to the date of a particular periodical. But, due to the enormous space newspapers and magazines take up, as well as the problem of decay, libraries only keep them for a limited time period and most of the older publications are only available on the library computer.

Librarians can assist you with online research beyond the usual Google or Yahoo! search engines. Westlaw, LexisNexis, other academic or scholarly search engines, and online databases may offer more in-depth or subject-specific research opportunities for your project or assignment.

# FIND SOURCES

Once you've discovered a source, you need to track it down. Use the best library that is available to you. A college or university library will probably have a more extensive collection and better resources than a local public library. However, the main branch of the public library in most cities will also have a large collection of sources and varied services.

The bulk of the library's resources consists of books that are shelved in the stacks. If you are looking for a book, simply check the library's catalog to find the call number. The first few digits of the call number will generally indicate the subject and its corresponding section of the library, while the last few digits indicate the book itself. Using the call number, you can find the exact shelf where a book should be located. You then just need to match the call number you've written down to the one on the spine of the library book. If you aren't certain where to look, ask the librarian. At almost all libraries, the public is allowed access to the stacks. You can freely look through the shelves for books you want to take out. At some institutions, however, you will need to fill out a request slip with the call number and give it to the librarian. A staff member will then retrieve the book for you.

Of course, a particular book is not always going to be on the shelf. Someone may have checked the book out or lost it. If this is the case, go to the circulation desk and tell them what you need. They can often tell you when the book is due back and put a hold on it so it will be reserved for you once it is returned. If the book is lost, they can place a search on it. If the book is missing, you should probably assume it is not going to be found and look for other sources.

If the library doesn't have a particular title, don't despair. Many libraries provide an interlibrary loan service through which you can borrow books from other libraries. Ask at the circulation desk or in the reference library for what you need to do to get a book through this service.

# DOCUMENT SOURCES

When conducting research, it is important to know how to categorize and document all of your sources. You also need to stay organized and have a good system to keep track of all the places where you gather your information. This system will ultimately protect you from committing plagiarism, whether accidentally or intentionally. Cite your sources.

Whenever you find a reference to a source you would like to investigate, make a note of it. It is extremely important that you write down all relevant information: the author(s), title, and publisher (for a book), volume and date (for a periodical or journal), or anthology name and editor (for an essay or article included in another work). This information will help you document the source and is also necessary when you create your own bibliography. You can keep this information in a notebook, on a legal pad, or in a file on your laptop.

# TAKE NOTES

When you are reading a particular source, you may not be certain what is relevant for you to document. Sources can be quite long, so how do you know what is useful and what isn't? Always make sure to look for anything that supports your thesis statement. Essentially, you are looking for evidence that will help you argue in favor of your thesis. You can also take notes on anything that relates to your general topic, since these notes will help you develop broad background knowledge of the field and might be used in the essay. Also, take notes on anything that intrigues you or sounds interesting. You won't necessarily use all of these notes in the essay, but it is much easier to write things down and throw them out later than to have to reread sources later on because you didn't take sufficient notes.

# NARROW YOUR TOPIC

In the initial stages of research, you may not have fully formulated your thesis or developed all of the overall points your essay will make. Therefore you may be uncertain about what notes to take. It can be helpful to read a small sampling of the sources you have tracked down before beginning to take notes. This will enable you to develop background knowledge on the subject, which, in turn, will help you fine-tune your thesis. When you have a better idea of the shape of your essay, you can then go back to various sources, read them carefully, and take notes.

By the way, if your essay uses primary sources, you need to read these carefully and make sure to take thorough notes on them. Notes and quotations from primary sources are particularly strong pieces of evidence, especially if a primary source is the focus of your essay.

# WRITE DOWN SPECIFIC INFORMATION

There are two ways of using gathered information in your essay: *quotations* and *paraphrases*. A quotation restates a passage or a part of a passage from a source in the original writer's *exact words*. A paraphrase, on the other hand, rephrases the ideas in a passage in *your own words*.

When you are reading a source and come across a sentence or passage you think is relevant, decide whether you want to quote it or paraphrase it. You should generally paraphrase more often than you quote. It is too tedious and time-consuming to copy down long passages word-for-word.

# QUOTE STRONGER PASSAGES

If a sentence or passage is written in a particularly interesting or powerful manner, you might think that it can stand well on its own. In this case, copy it as a quotation. Be certain that you put copied lines in quotation marks. You might even want to write "Quotation from Original" next to the line in parentheses. If you want to leave out part of a quotation because it is irrelevant, you can use an *ellipsis* to indicate a word or phrase has been deleted. An ellipsis consists of either three spaced periods if the omission is within a sentence, or four spaced periods if the omission comes at the end of a sentence (since the first dot represents the period at the end of the sentence). Sometimes, when you take a quotation out of context, it won't make sense on its own and will need some clarification. If you decide to add a word or phrase to the quotation, you must put the addition in brackets to indicate that the added material is not part of the original quotation.

# PARAPHRASING

If you decide to paraphrase the source, you must rephrase it *in your own words*. Be certain that your paraphrase is an accurate restatement of the passage. Occasionally, you will want to quote a few words or a particular phrase within a paraphrase. You can paraphrase the gist of the passage and include only a few words and phrases in quotation marks. For example, if the author has coined a particular term or described something in a unique way, you can quote those words exactly. Whenever you take quotes from a source, and even if you paraphrase them, you need to note the source and its exact page number(s). It is important that you do this carefully, as you must include this information later in the essay. If you don't acknowledge the original source, you are committing *plagiarism*, which is considered a serious breach of ethics that can get you expelled from school.

# USE NOTE CARDS OR OTHER METHODS

If you are using many sources and taking many notes, the material can become difficult to manage. An efficient and organized means of taking notes is to use note cards. These give you more flexibility—you can shuffle and reorganize them into various groups, or put aside those you decide not to use. Take notes on index cards (you may want to use a slightly larger size, such as 4" × 6", so you can fit more notes). On each card, write down a particular piece of information from one source.

Each card should contain a single, specific idea. Copying lengthy quotations or paraphrasing large chunks of text takes away the flexibility that note cards provide in the first place, so try to limit each card to a single point. Keep careful records with complete publication information of all your sources. In order to credit the sources, you need to place a "works-cited" page at the end of your essay that includes all this information.

Using works-cited note cards is the most efficient way to keep track of sources. Simply keep one note card per source, complete with all its bibliographic information. Alphabetize the cards at the end and format them properly depending on the type of publication source (a book, website, periodical, speech, etc.). As long as you have made works-cited cards, you don't need to put the full title and complete publication information on each. Simply copy down the last name of the author in the upper left-hand corner. If you are using more than one source by a particular writer, you can write down the author's last name and a key word from the title. In the top right-hand corner, write down the exact page number from which the noted quotation or paraphrase comes.

Another way to take notes is to use a notebook or legal pad as you read, but some students prefer to take notes directly onto a laptop or desktop computer. Find a system that works for you. Remember to indicate clearly which source the notes come from and the page numbers.

# GENERATE YOUR OWN IDEAS

Regardless of whether you are required to conduct research, the heart of *your own* essay should be *your own* ideas. In the course of researching and thinking about your topic, you will develop certain ideas and a sense of the major points you want to make.

The writing process is like brainstorming; as you write about one particular idea or point, you'll probably find yourself developing many additional ones. You don't need to worry about things like grammar, spelling, format, or structure when you write down your ideas. You don't even have to write in complete sentences! Just scribble down anything that comes to mind about your topic. You can then refer to these notes as you organize your essay.

When you are finished jotting down your ideas, read them over and transfer the major ones onto note cards. You can play around with how you organize them in this form, and you can also integrate them with your note cards about outside sources. Write a key word or phrase to describe each category on an index card so you can identify each group. If a card seems to belong in more than one group, place it in the one that seems most applicable; however, write a note on the card indicating the other categories where it could belong.

After going through your notes, you'll have several piles of note cards made up of various categories and subcategories of notes. Each group represents a point you plan to make in the essay. Next, you need to decide on the order in which you will address these points. How you structure your essay is a personal decision. Different writers have their own favorite strategic devices and techniques. Likewise, each essay has its own logic. Before you start writing, consider the overall effect you want to create and think of a way to achieve it.

# PLAGIARISM 101

As you research and generate your own ideas, it's vital to avoid plagiarism. So what exactly is it?

Plagiarism is a form of academic stealing. Whenever one writer uses another writer's ideas or words and does not give the original writer credit, it is considered plagiarism. Committing plagiarism is a breach of ethics that can have serious repercussions for a student, ranging from a failing grade to expulsion.

The most blatant form of plagiarism is copying an entire essay from another student or source. It is also considered plagiarism if you include information from another source within your essay and don't credit the source. Even one sentence or phrase without attribution can be considered plagiarism. You probably won't be expelled over one or two such sentences, but failing to document sources can significantly lower your grade and cast doubt on you as a student. Committing plagiarism is an infraction that can haunt you for years, as it often becomes a part of your permanent academic record. It is so much better to be conservative and cite anything that is not your own work, idea, or quotation than to risk getting tagged as a plagiarist.

## GIVE CREDIT WHERE CREDIT IS DUE

When you are assigned an essay that requires research, you are obviously allowed to consult sources.

As you might imagine, quoting from, paraphrasing, and crediting sources can become quite messy, especially if you aren't consistent about the way you do it. To help make essays readable, standard formats have been developed to provide consistency within an essay and from one essay to another. Ask your professor which format to use and be certain you follow it.

Currently the most popular ways of citing sources in almost all schools are those developed by the Modern Language Association (MLA) and American Psychological Association (APA). They are known as the MLA and APA formats, and you can purchase a handbook for either one. (There are also websites like *www.noodlebib.com* that format your citations for you if you plug in the title, author, publisher, etc.)

In general, these standard formats consist of two components: citations within the essay and the list of works cited at the essay's conclusion. Whenever you quote or paraphrase a source, include a citation with the sentence or passage that indicates the source and page number. These citations are usually abbreviations for the whole source, such as the author's last name or a key word in the source's title. The citation corresponds to a listing in the works-cited section at the end of the essay, where the full publication information for each source is listed. There are specific formats for listing different types of sources in the works-cited section. Your professor will specify a specific format, and you can purchase a handbook to help you with it. Remember, always give credit where credit is due.

# CHAPTER 6

# SUMMARY

» The crucial component of good essay writing is the quality and strength of your ideas.

» Select a topic that excites or interests you.

» Your writing is one of the most direct forms of communication between you and your teacher. What your teacher sees in your writing contributes significantly to the impression she has of you.

» Review the suggestions offered for how to start your writing assignment.

» Once you've chosen a topic, immerse yourself in the subject matter by reading and thinking about it.

» Create a strong thesis statement that serves as the core component of your essay.

» Find a strong title for your essay.

» Become a researcher who seeks ideas of others to confirm or deny your thesis statement or assigned topic.

» Use your local library and don't be afraid to ask the librarian for help.

» Track down and properly document your sources.

» Follow the suggested guidelines to narrow your topic and take good notes.

» Use note cards and find a system of note taking that works well for you.

» Plagiarizing is the equivalent of academic stealing. Do not plagiarize.

# WRITE COMPELLING ESSAYS

Before lawyers go to court, they carefully prepare for how they will present their evidence. They think about the order in which they plan to call witnesses and the particular lines of questioning they will follow. Planning ahead in this way guarantees an organized and strategically effective presentation of the case. Similarly, your essay represents an argument—this one in support of your thesis. Like a lawyer, you also need to plan ahead, organizing your evidence and devising a presentation strategy.

# PLAN YOUR ATTACK

The first thing to do is to read through and evaluate all your notes. Decide which of them are necessary for your argument. *Everything in the final essay must relate to the thesis statement*. You may ultimately decide to put many unrelated notes aside; don't let this bother you. If you evaluate notes in a critical manner, only the most powerful material will remain. Information that doesn't contribute significantly weighs down the essay and detracts from the stronger ideas, so it must be deleted.

As you work, keep your own ideas in mind. You may want to use them as the basis for grouping together the themes. Each group of note cards you wrote represents a point you plan to make in the essay.

Next you need to decide on the order in which you will address these points. Many students follow some variation of the following steps of the writing process.

» Brainstorming
» Starting an Outline
» Writing the First Draft

# BRAINSTORMING

On a blank sheet of paper or computer screen, you can brainstorm some of your ideas and see how they come together. Some students like to "cluster" to come up with a more formal outline. "Clustering" is a visual way of mapping out your future essay. If your essay is about water, for instance, write the word "water" in the center of a page. Then, branching out around it like the rays of a sun, write various words or terms that support, define, or relate to the topic of water.

Another technique that can get your structure on paper is "freewriting." This is simply a stream-of-consciousness way to write ideas down as they jump into your head. Ignoring sentence structure, grammar, and spelling, you just write without stopping until you empty your head of ideas for your essay.

## STARTING AN OUTLINE

When you plan your essay, it helps to make a rough outline. The outline lists the major points of the essay, and the smaller topics and issues that relate to each one, in the order in which you plan to address them. This gives you a clear map to follow when you sit down to write. Like all good maps, it will keep you from getting lost.

Try to include as much detail as possible within the rough outline. The more specifics you include, the more organized you'll be. Beneath the general categories in the outline, you can mention specific notes from sources you plan to use, and you might even want to write out or sum up specific quotations. When organizing your points, be certain that you order them in a logical fashion. You want one point to lead to the next, so that the reader will be able to follow your argument without having to fill in gaps. Certain categories of notes should follow one another. The order in which you bring up points can influence the effect they have on your reader.

In evaluating your different notes (your pieces of "evidence"), you've probably become aware that certain ones are much more powerful than others. Order your points so that the most persuasive ones pack the most punch. You may want to build up to your most powerful point so you make a strong last impression on your reader. At the same time, you don't want to start off with a weak point that will make a poor first impression.

Remember that this rough outline is not written in stone; you can make changes at any time. In the process of writing the essay, or after you've read over early drafts of it, you may find that certain points work better if they are addressed in a different place in the essay. You can make as many changes as you like, provided that everything in the essay still relates to the thesis.

# WRITING THE FIRST DRAFT

The most important goal of a first (or rough) draft is to get all your ideas on paper and to integrate them with notes from other sources. Correct grammar and spelling are important parts of an essay because they help make it understandable and readable. However, don't concern yourself with this in your first draft. This practice eliminates a great deal of the stress about writing; you don't have to think about the "rules" at first and can simply concentrate on conveying your ideas.

Start at the beginning of the rough outline and write. Do your best to explain each of the points. Refer to your notes and include quotations or paraphrases from other sources as needed. Be certain you add citations for each sentence that includes information from another source. Keep on writing until you've reached the end of the rough outline. Don't stop to go back or make changes. If you hit a roadblock—a point when you freeze and don't know how to proceed—mark the place with an *X* and move on to another point. You can go back to the trouble spot later. This first draft will be extremely rough; the writing will be choppy and difficult to read. But that's okay—it's only the first draft and you are the only one who has to see it. This draft provides you with the raw material for your essay; you can then work on it and refine it until it is a real gem.

# FIVE-PARAGRAPH ESSAY STRUCTURE

Although there are many ways to structure an essay, the most basic is the five-paragraph structure that includes an introduction with thesis statement, three supporting paragraphs, and conclusion. There's no law that you have to use this structure for everything you write. You might, for example, have a teacher who is open to more loosely structured essays and who encourages you to be creative. But regardless of how lenient the teacher is, this structure is a basic fundamental formula that, if mastered, can take you through high school and college quite effectively. It ensures that the essay remains focused on a specific point and that ideas are presented in a logical and organized fashion. Following this structure, especially when you are first learning how to write academic essays, will help you write more persuasively. In the next few pages we outline the five-paragraph essay structure.

# THE INTRODUCTION

The introduction is where you present your general topic, specific thesis statement, and approach or methodology. For most essays, the introduction only needs to be a single, well-written paragraph. By being short and sweet, the introduction has more impact.

The introduction should draw your reader into your argument right away. It functions somewhat like a movie preview, giving your audience a taste of what's to come, but not the whole story. You want to entice your reader in what you have to say. In a bigger project or longer writing assignment (more than twenty pages) such as an honors thesis or dissertation, the introduction can be longer than a paragraph since there is more ground to cover and a larger set of topics to introduce.

Because the thesis statement is central to the essay, it is an important part of the introduction. You generally can't begin an essay with the thesis statement itself, because it represents a specific point of view about a broader subject. The introduction sets up the thesis by presenting general background information that gives the thesis statement context.

Begin the introductory paragraph with a broad, general statement (or question) about the paper's topic. Try to have this "hook" sentence be interesting and catchy so you can encourage your reader to continue reading. Remember that the beginning few sentences give the reader the first impression of your essay and it is extremely important that you make it a good one. The first sentences should be well written, interesting, and, most importantly, give the reader some idea of the paper's topic. The rest of the introduction then bridges the opening statement with the thesis statement, which is usually the last sentence of the introduction.

In your introduction, you should indicate how you plan to approach your argument and the kinds of sources that will serve as your evidence. If you plan on looking at specific examples to prove the thesis, you can also identify these cases. The introduction is the place in the essay where you first spell out the thesis statement directly for the reader. You therefore need to be careful about how you word it. You don't want it to be too fancy, flashy, or wordy; the power of the idea should be enough to impress the reader. Just state it in a direct, unambiguous manner.

In general, this is not the place to quote and paraphrase outside sources. Those sources belong in the body of the paper, where you use them to prove the thesis statement. It wouldn't make any sense to discuss such specific sources before you've even stated the argument of the essay. Moreover, you want the reader to be impressed by the power of your own ideas.

# START OFF STRONG

Like the introduction, the first sentence of your essay must capture the reader's attention. Look at the first lines of your favorite books or read the opening phrases of classic novels for inspiration on how to begin your paper. Don't be afraid to take risks—find creative ways to "hook" your reader. Sometimes, you can also begin an essay with a quotation from another source; however, you should only do this if the quotation is closely connected to your thesis statement. If the quotation introduces specific issues, you probably should not use it early in the essay. If you want to be a bit more creative with the introduction and you think your teacher is open to a less standard kind of writing, you could start the essay with a brief observation or question that relates to your topic. Just remember that the opening sentence should always be strong, as it is the first chance to really "wow" your reader.

# THE BODY

The body is the bulk of your essay; this is where you present your detailed argument that supports the thesis statement. After having conducted research and thought about your topic, you should have several good points you want to make in your essay. You will use the body paragraphs to present these ideas in a clear and organized fashion.

If you have conducted research from primary or secondary sources, you can quote and paraphrase from these sources in this part of the essay. Information that comes from other sources serves as strong evidence, but make sure that you distinguish your own ideas from those in other sources. Quotations and paraphrases should only be brought in to give your ideas credibility. Whenever you introduce information from another source, you should explain exactly how it fits in with your own point. Moreover always be certain that each time you quote or paraphrase an outside source, you formally credit the source using the *MLA Handbook for Writers of Research Papers* as your reference for proper formatting and crediting of sources.

As you write, make sure your paragraphs aren't too long. Long paragraphs weigh down your essay, and your reader will find it tedious if you drone on and on about a supporting idea. Sprinkle in quotes or a thought-provoking question to help provide lively content. Each sentence in the body paragraphs should flow smoothly and logically. Use transition words and phrases in certain sentences, particularly topic sentences, so that your reader can easily follow how different points are related to one another. There are many transition words and phrases you can use to connect various sentences and paragraphs, including these:

» To build upon a previous sentence or paragraph: *and, also, additionally, as a result, consequently, further, furthermore, in addition, moreover*

» To compare with a previous sentence or paragraph: *similarly, in the same manner, likewise, at the same time, by the same token*

» To contrast with a previous sentence or paragraph: *however, but, in contrast, nevertheless, although, yet, on the other hand*

» To summarize or draw a conclusion: *therefore, in other words, in short, to sum up, thus*

# THE CONCLUSION

After reading the body of your essay and all the evidence you've presented in support of the thesis, the reader should now view the thesis statement as a claim that has been all but proven. Your conclusion is your last chance to sum up your arguments and assert the validity of your thesis.

This section of the essay is essentially the mirror image of the introduction, but it stresses the fact that the thesis has now been proven. You should also recap the major points you've made in the paper. Like the introduction, the conclusion of most essays only needs to be one paragraph, and it should be composed of mainly your own words and ideas. This is not a place to quote or paraphrase extensively from secondary sources.

While the introduction contributes to the reader's first impression of your essay, the conclusion will influence the reader's final impression. You want to end with a bang—with some of your most powerful and dramatic writing—that leaves the reader absolutely convinced that your argument is valid. The most basic conclusion starts off with a restatement of the thesis statement and then sums up the essay's main ideas with general statements. The final sentence is a broad remark about the subject or topic.

This standard format can vary in some instances. Depending on the freedom your teacher allows, you might also try to be more creative in the conclusion. No matter the form of the conclusion, the same general rule applies: the conclusion should bring the essay to a formal close and show that the thesis statement has been proven.

# SPECIAL ESSAY TYPES

Your teachers may ask you to write many types of essays. Besides the traditional five-paragraph format, you might have to write a persuasive essay, an expository paper, a personal statement, or a research paper. The following entries familiarize you with more specific forms of writing. No matter the type of essay, though, you must always remember the different stages of writing: *think, research, organize, draft, revise, edit,* and *proofread.*

# PERSUASIVE ESSAY

A persuasive essay, also known as an argumentative essay, persuades the reader to believe in a concept by convincing him that the concept is true. Just as a lawyer argues his case to the jury, your writing will argue your idea so that the reader comes away agreeing with you, or at least questioning what he may otherwise have believed.

Writing a persuasive essay requires you to use vocabulary and sentences that exude confidence; your word choice should be certain and strong, affirming and reaffirming your belief in your cause. Words and phrases such as *certainly, definitively, in fact, confidently, with conviction,* and *beyond a shadow of a doubt* will help convince your reader to believe in the point you are trying to prove.

Formatting your persuasive essay is similar to formatting the five-paragraph essay: introduction, supporting paragraphs, and a conclusion. However, one of your body paragraphs should offer the opposing view of what you are trying to say. By doing this, you state the opposition and face it head-on. This way, you build your credibility with the reader since you are not afraid to face the opposition. However, be sure that you refute the opposition's argument, showing that the opposition is still not as strong as your argument. Your essay should read like a well-organized conversation you are having with your reader; the tone should be strong, accessible, and confident. Thus, each sentence should be written with conviction to set a tone of certainty and confidence in your assertion or opinion.

# EXPOSITORY WRITING

Like the five-paragraph and persuasive essays, expository essays consist of a thesis, supporting paragraphs, and a conclusion. What makes expository writing different is that it does not present your opinion or feelings about your topic. Rather, it responds to a factual prompt (such as a question from history or a scientific explanation for an event or experiment) or request for basic information (such as how to brush you teeth or program your DVR). Expository essays can also ask you to analyze or describe a process, idea, or event in time.

Expository essays are factual, not based on opinion. They often answer such questions as "how" or "why" something has happened or is what it is. This kind of essay does not offer the writer's point of view; it illuminates and analyzes the views of others matter-of-factly and without debating or arguing a subject.

# PERSONAL STATEMENT

- - - - - - - - - - - - - - - - - - - - - - - - - - - - -

When writing a personal statement, you can basically throw the rules of the five-paragraph essay out the window. That's because in terms of structure, tone, and concept the personal statement is about *you*: it is written in the first person on a topic that only you could write about.

Personal statements are used often for college or graduate school applications to allow the admission office an opportunity to get to know you better. Selecting a generic theme or topic is not a good idea for such essays. Dig deeper to find stories that are meaningful to you and that give the reader a glimpse of who you are. You will have an easier time piquing the interest of your reader and communicating your passion if you write about an experience, concept, conversation, challenge, or life moment that is meaningful to you. Here are some tips for writing a personal essay:

» You don't need to write about the most dramatic event of your life to separate yourself from the crowd. Good essays often stem from commonplace events.

» Feel free to use sentence fragments, pieces of dialogue or conversation, or humor if it suits you.

» Show more than you tell. Use examples instead of statements.

» Use your five senses when you write so your reader can see, hear, taste, smell, and feel your experience.

» Write in an authentic voice. Be open, honest, and always write in the first person.

» Practice reading your essay aloud or into a recorder. Does your essay sound like you? Is your voice coming through?

Be careful about seeking too much feedback from teachers, friends, or relatives. They can help you to determine if your voice is authentic, but they shouldn't give you ideas on what to write.

# RESEARCH PAPER

A research paper uses both outside sources and your own ideas to express information and support a particular point or topic. Research papers tend to be lengthier since they combine quotes from various sources with your thoughts and ideas about a particular subject.

Plan to spend many hours in the process of collecting, assimilating, distilling, and expressing information when you write a research paper. Whatever type of writing you are asked to do, be sure that you understand what your teacher expects of you in terms of length, number of outside sources needed, and, if applicable, particular sources you must use in addition to your own ideas. Also, be certain that you follow the assignment guidelines. Some teachers want students to learn how to use the library system to do research, rather than gathering all the information online.

# REVISIONS AND THE FINAL DRAFT

As you read and revise your first draft, try to think of yourself as an editor reading over an article for a newspaper. As an editor, it's your job to make sure that your target audience will be able to understand the article. You might also try reading the essay out loud, so you can hear how it sounds. At this stage, you do need to worry about correct grammar and spelling; eliminating grammatical or mechanical errors makes it easier for the reader to understand and appreciate your ideas.

Once you have completed your first draft, you should go back to the beginning and read it. Try to read your essay from a critical standpoint, as if you were someone else looking over your work. Because you are so closely tied to your ideas, this will be difficult; however, being objective helps you catch many errors that could have gone by undetected. As you read over the draft, ask yourself:

» Is everything explained fully?
» Will the reader understand the essay?
» Are there any holes or gaps in the argument?
» Are any ideas not fully developed or only partially explained?
» Does each idea flow smoothly into the next?
» What additional information does the reader need to appreciate my point?

Make appropriate notes based on what you just asked yourself. Try to anticipate questions a reader might have and write them in the margins.

# REWRITE YOUR DRAFT

Now you're ready to rewrite. As you go over your draft, answer the questions you have written in the margins, adding more information to the essay. Revise the piece as many times as necessary, until you're satisfied with it. The changes you make will improve the essay with each draft.

The first few times you read and rewrite, you should focus on the content—the ideas and points that are explained in the essay.

» As with the first draft, be certain all your ideas are clearly and fully explained, that nothing is ambiguous or partially stated, and that there are no gaps or holes.

» Examine the organization of your work and make sure that one point flows smoothly and logically into the next. You might try moving sections of the essay around to see if they work more effectively somewhere else.

» Be sure that everything in the essay supports the thesis statement, and take out anything that detracts from (or doesn't add to) the argument.

» Review individual sentences and paragraphs to ensure that your points are clear and cohesive.

» Think about ways you can rework sentences to make them clearer.

When you are reviewing your essay, be sure that you have met the page requirements set by your teacher. Remember, the best way to ensure that your essay will be the appropriate length is to choose the right topic. Once you've started writing, you may find your essay is a bit longer or shorter than you intended. If your essay is only half a page longer or shorter, most professors will still accept it. If it is off by more than half a page, then you need to make adjustments.

# PROOFREAD! PROOFREAD! PROOFREAD!

Always proofread your essay before turning it in. Proofreading is different from rewriting, because when you proofread, you are looking for errors in grammar, spelling, mechanics, punctuation, and style. You can often find it difficult to catch these errors, because being accustomed to the essay as it stands, you simply do not see them. In order to proofread effectively, you need to read in a much more focused manner.

If you feel comfortable doing so, give your paper to a close friend, mentor, or teacher (not the one who assigned the paper, though!). Sometimes fresh eyes can make you see things you missed or may not have considered. Conversely, beware that too many reviewers can take your voice out of the work you created. So pick and choose the feedback you receive and do not second-guess your instincts.

When you are ready, print out a clean copy of the essay. Bring it to a location where there are absolutely no distractions. It is extremely important that the entire time you read, you keep in your mind that you are trying to locate errors. If you forget this and get caught up in the content of the essay, you will continue to overlook mistakes. Read slowly and methodically, concentrating on each word. It is extremely helpful to read out loud, so that you can hear each word; if you're someplace where this is impossible (such as a library), you can also simply mouth the words silently. Hearing your words out loud can also help you identify where you may need to add or take away commas, semi-colons, or periods.

# SPELL-CHECK ISN'T ALWAYS WRIGHT

Spell-check and grammar-checking mechanisms built into your computer's word-processing software do not catch every error. So don't rely solely on a computer to find your mistakes. Printing out your paper and reading a hard copy makes it easier to see mistakes that you may not catch on your computer screen. Your computer's spell-check program is helpful and can correct many errors, but it does not catch everything and it does not understand the misuse of a word. The spell-check will not catch homophones like, *to*, *two*, and *too*—words that sound the same but have different meanings. Just like with proofreading, consider finding a friend, upperclassman, family member, or mentor to read your work in its final stage so that he can offer comments or edits if he encounters any errors you may have missed.

# GRAMMAR IS ESSENTIAL

Your voice is important to your essay and your thesis statement is central to your argument but how can someone understand either if you use poor grammar? Your ideas are a key component to any essay; without strong ideas, an essay will not be impressive, no matter how well written it might be. But correct grammar is just as important—it is what makes your writing understandable and direct.

There are many different grammar rules. You can't possibly memorize them all, and you shouldn't try. As a child you did not learn to speak by learning the "rules" of conversation; you picked up the language by listening to others. You can also learn about grammar and usage by reading. The more you read, the more you will develop an ear for correct grammar. When you write, something will "sound" right or wrong to you. Try to read more frequently and trust your ear for correct usage. If you have a serious problem with grammar, though, you may consider working with a peer or paid tutor.

## TAKE ONE LAST LOOK

Read the final version of your essay to make sure that it is clean, neat, and correct. Correct any typos or other imperfections and print the essay out again, if necessary. Include your name and the page number on each page, and staple the pages together. Either on the first page or on a title page, you should also include your name, the professor's name, the name of the course, and the title of your essay. However, if your teacher has a specific way of formatting the first page, follow her rules. In any case, the title should make the essay's topic very clear to the reader. You can, though, be a bit creative with the title to make the topic sound interesting and provocative. After you've completed editing, proofreading, and formatting the essay, print out the final version and turn it in!

## CHAPTER 7

# SUMMARY

» Brainstorm and plan your writing project before you begin. Try "clustering," or "freewriting" to get your ideas flowing.

» Start an outline to use as your roadmap for your assignment.

» Write a first draft to get your ideas down. Don't aim for perfection.

» Learn and master the five-paragraph essay structure: introduction, body or supporting paragraphs, and conclusion. Start off with a strong hook, support your ideas, and tie the whole piece together with a tidy conclusion.

» A persuasive essay, also known as an argumentative essay, is an essay that persuades the reader to believe in a concept by convincing the reader that the concept is true.

» An expository essay does not present your opinion or feelings about your topic. Rather, it responds to a factual prompt or request for basic information.

» A research paper uses both outside sources and your own ideas to express information and support a particular point or topic.

» Plan to revise and rework your essay as you incorporate feedback or look at it later with fresh eyes. Revise the first draft as many times as necessary, until you're satisfied with it.

» Always proofread your essay. Look for errors in grammar, spelling, mechanics, punctuation, and style.

» Don't trust that spell-check or grammar-checking mechanisms built into your computer's word-processing software are always correct. They do not catch every error!

» Use correct grammar—it is what makes your writing understandable and direct.

» Take one last look at the final version of your essay to make sure that it is clean, neat, and correct. Then turn it in!

# STUDY EFFECTIVELY

As a student, you are faced with many tasks, activities, and responsibilities. This load can be overwhelming. The key to making it all manageable is making much of it a matter of habit. You need to adopt an effective study routine for everything you do.

The more routine something is, the less effort it requires. Think about your morning ritual. You probably go through the same activities every day—showering, brushing your teeth, getting dressed—without thinking about it. If you also make study tasks a habit, they'll become as easy as brushing your teeth.

Begin by creating an effective study space. Not every student studies and gets work done in the same manner. Some of your classmates may need to come home, turn on the TV, have a snack, and relax before they get to the grind of homework. Others go straight to extracurricular activities, rush to an after-school job or volunteer work, come home for dinner, and then begin homework. Still others use free blocks during the school day to get a head start on studying or homework. Whatever your style or routine may be, find a system to get your work done.

The space that you choose is crucial to your success as a student. Make sure the spot where you do your work is well lit, free from distractions (like a cell phone or a computer, which can distract you with instant messages, the Internet, and e-mail), and is an environment where you can successfully get your work done. Determine what type of environment is most suitable for your academic success, then discipline yourself to keep your area in that condition.

## FIGURING OUT WHAT WORKS FOR YOU

Do you prefer quiet solitude in a corner of a library? Do you stay on task with a buddy and use this social factor as part of your homework or study routine? Do you prefer to break your work into smaller chunks? Some coursework lends itself more easily to group or dialogue-based studying. Other subjects require deeper concentration and memorization. Find a strategy that suits your learning style and stay consistent.

Many people seem to think that the only way to study is at a bare desk, with a hard-backed chair, in a minuscule cubicle in the library. While this setting *does* wipe out any outside distraction, it's such a gloomy atmosphere that studying turns into a form of medieval torture. Studying doesn't have to be that depressing. Since you will spend long hours doing homework or reading over your notes and assigned texts, you may as well make yourself comfortable. If you work in a space where you are relaxed and feel at home, you will study more often and more effectively.

Study anywhere you feel comfortable (e.g., in your room, in bed, at the library, in an empty classroom, at a café, outside, in the park) provided that you do two things: minimize outside distractions, and promise yourself to make a change if you don't get the work done. When choosing a place to study, consider the number of outside distractions—such as friends' stopping by or a phone that is ringing—and do what you can to minimize them. Even the library may not be distraction-free. If everyone you know goes there to study, you may spend more time chatting with friends than studying. You can, though, minimize the distraction by avoiding the main study lounge and finding a quieter section of the library, where you won't run into many people you know.

## STUDYING IN YOUR ROOM

There's nothing wrong with studying in your room, as long as you get work done. Your room is, after all, the space where you are most at home. Again, minimize diversions. If you are frequently interrupted by the phone, siblings, friends, roommates, or instant messaging, turn off your phone or computer. If friends or siblings frequently disturb you, keep the door closed.

If you decide to study in your room, it's a good idea to designate a spot as your main workspace. Your desk is probably the best place. Occasionally, you can listen to music while you study, just as long as it doesn't distract you. Listening to something old that you are very familiar with will divert you less than newly released tunes that make you want to learn the lyrics. If you study outside your room, you can bring your iPod along. That's one way to make wherever you study feel a little more like home.

# DON'T FALL ASLEEP ON THE JOB

Whatever your learning style might be, it is important that you stay awake and alert when you study. This might sound like a joke, but falling asleep while reading or studying is a problem that plagues many students. The need to sleep is strong—and to fight it, you must take equally strong measures. Here are a few important suggestions:

» Get enough sleep. Try to get six to eight hours of sleep every night.
» Don't get too much sleep. If you get much more sleep than your body needs, you can feel sleepy all day long.
» Exercise regularly. If you do that, you'll sleep better at night and be more energized during the day. Oxygen will flow through your body better. That means you'll be more alert and focused on your classes and your studies.
» Use an alarm. If you can't set it to go off regularly, set it for a specific time (such as a half hour after you've begun studying) and continue to reset it each time it goes off.
» Schedule wake-up calls or visits. If you don't trust an alarm, have a friend check on you.
» Take breathers. If you become too comfortable while studying, it's easy to fall asleep. You should plan to get up and walk around outside at regular intervals.

» Stay actively involved. The more engaged in the material you are, the less likely you'll fall asleep. Rather than just reading the words on the page, have a conversation in your mind about what you read. Read a few lines and then comment on them.

» Don't get too comfortable. Avoid clothing that is too warm or cozy. In other words, don't wear clothes that feel too much like pajamas.

# BE ORGANIZED

Being a student is tougher than some nine-to-five office jobs because your responsibilities and duties are constantly changing. Every day, every week, every month, and every semester presents new assignments and tasks, and if you don't keep track of them, you'll find that your work becomes a complete mess. That's why it's essential that you are always organized. In addition to keeping track of your responsibilities on your calendar, you should also keep all of your notes and study materials neatly organized.

There's no point in taking notes if they wind up in a crumpled pile of paper at the back of your desk. Keep your notes clearly labeled and organized. Find a space that you can designate as your study area, where you keep all the study materials—notes, textbooks, articles—that you need for the semester. That way you'll be able to quickly find anything you need.

Another way to stay organized is to break down larger projects into smaller pieces. For example, if you have a huge book report and presentation to finish, make a timeline and cut the project into pieces by focusing on one section at a time (e.g., introduction, supporting paragraphs, conclusion, references and bibliography, project visuals, examples and illustrations of text, etc.)

# USE FLASH CARDS FOR MEMORIZATION

The most effective way to memorize key terms is to work with good, old-fashioned flash cards. Flash cards are particularly helpful when you need to remember a lot of key terms, such as new vocabulary words in a foreign language. Simply take 3" × 5" index cards and write down a term on one side and either a definition, a description of its significance, or a translation on the other.

Although making the flash cards might seem time-consuming, this method has many advantages. First, the process of making the cards helps you start memorizing the material. As you write down a term and its definition, your mind begins to file the information into your long-term memory. Second, using cards allows you to shuffle and reorganize your flash cards in various ways. For example, you can eliminate cards for terms you know well, and continue to test yourself on the ones you don't. Third, flash cards enable you to quiz yourself in two ways: you can look at the term and test yourself on the definition or look at the definition and try to guess the term. If you can do both, then you truly know the material. This can particularly help on those questions where you need to supply the term instead of the definition, such as with fill-in-the-blank questions. For this reason, flash cards are also useful in preparing for exams on foreign language vocabulary where you need to know both the English definition of a word and the foreign word itself to answer questions.

Flash cards make it easy for you to test yourself on key terms. Quiz yourself often. Sit with the stack of cards and, for each one, state the definition or description of the term. Then flip the card over to see if you were correct. If you were right and feel confident that you won't forget the term, put the card aside. If you got it wrong or had trouble describing it in detail, put the card at the bottom of the stack. Before you do, though, read over the card a few times and make a concentrated effort to remember it. When you have finished going through the whole stack, shuffle the cards and start again. Repeat the process, continuing to eliminate any cards you find you know quite well.

# IMPROVE YOUR MEMORY

Some people are gifted with photographic memories. They can read a passage of a text and then repeat it word-for-word from memory. Most people, though, find it very difficult to memorize information. Like listening, memorizing takes effort. There are, however, a number of strategies to help you improve your memory. These are known as *mnemonic devices*.

Many people think that if they stare at a word, text, or image long enough, they will remember it. They think that by staring at something, they have probably succeeded at inputting the information into their long-term memory. The trouble comes later on, when they try to retrieve that information. Long-term memory is somewhat like a large closet—it can hold an awful lot—but as you put more and more into it, it becomes harder to find exactly what you want. Mnemonic devices function as trigger mechanisms that conjure more detailed information from your long-term memory. Rhymes, alliteration, mental associations, visualizations, acronyms, and repeated exposure all help your memory work to its maximum potential.

# ALWAYS ALLITERATE

A series of two or more words that begin with the same letter or sound (such as "King Kong" or "Peter Piper picked a peck of pickled peppers") is alliteration. To use alliteration as a mnemonic device, take whatever key term you are trying to memorize and find some word beginning with the same sound that will trigger information about the term. For example, let's say you were trying to memorize the meaning of the word *plethora*, which according to the dictionary means excess or abundance. You can associate *plethora* with *plenty*. And since both *plethora* and *plenty* begin with the letter *P* (in fact, they both begin with the sound *pl*), it will be much easier to remember the word *plenty* than *abundance*. The word *plenty* makes you think of having too much of something—in other words, an abundance.

# MAKE MENTAL ASSOCIATIONS

Another mnemonic device is called *mental association*. Think of a word or image you associate with both the term and its definition: this association functions as a link between the term and the information you hope to remember about it. For example, if you want to remember that Edison created the light bulb, you can look at Edison's name and see the word *son* in it. *Son* sounds just like *sun*, so you can associate Edison's name with the sun. The sun, of course, is a source of light. So, by linking Edison with the sun, you can bring to mind the image of light and the light bulb. Similarly, if you wanted to remember that the tiny, wispy clouds in the sky are called *cirrus* clouds, you could associate the wisps in the sky with horse's tails. Horses are found in the *circus* which sounds like *cirrus*.

When you try to create these mental associations, it's often helpful to rely on your personal experiences. For example, one student who needed to remember that *Luncheon of the Boating Party* was painted by Auguste Renoir had visited her aunt's lake house in August. She remembered that she had ridden in her aunt's boat, and associated the boat in August with *Luncheon of the Boating Party* by Auguste Renoir. You can get as creative as you want in finding these associations. If necessary, you can think up a detailed, elaborate story that will help you link a word with information about it. These stories can be as silly, illogical, or personal as you like, just as long as they work. A mental association only needs to make sense to you; you don't have to feel obliged to share it with other people.

# VISUALIZE TO MEMORIZE

You've probably heard the expression, "A picture is worth a thousand words." Well, it's also much easier to remember pictures than words. Therefore, you can use mental images and pictures instead of words and phrases to help you remember something. For example, one way to associate two or more words together is to create a picture in your mind that connects them. For example, if you want to remember that John Keats wrote "Ode on a Grecian Urn," you might picture an urn filled with enormous *keys* (which sounds like *Keats*) inside of it.

Visualizations can be particularly helpful when you need to associate several different terms or images. If you want to remember that the Department of Agriculture is part of the president's cabinet, you can picture a stalk of corn inside of a large, oak cabinet. You can then add to that image by placing other objects in the cabinet to indicate other departments in the president's cabinet, such as a giant penny to indicate the Treasury, a gun to indicate Defense, and even a schoolbook to indicate the Department of Education.

# A.C.R.O.N.Y.M.S.

An acronym is a word that is formed by taking the first letters from several words in a series, such as SCUBA: S(elf) C(ontained) U(nderwater) B(reathing) A(pparatus). Acronyms can be instrumental in helping you remember a long list of items, especially if you need to remember them in a particular order. For example, to remember the colors of the rainbow, many students memorize the name Roy G. Biv, an acronym made by taking the first letter of each color of the rainbow in order: R(ed), O(range), Y(ellow), G(reen), B(lue), I(ndigo), V(iolet). PEMDAS, another commonly used acronym, helps math students learn the order of operations: P(arentheses), E(xponents), M(ultiplication), D(ivision), A(ddition), S(ubtraction). Sometimes, however, the first letters of each word do not make a simple, easy-to-remember acronym like Roy G. Biv or PEMDAS. In those cases, you can create an entire sentence where the first letter of each word in the sentence corresponds to the first letter of the items you are memorizing.

## REPEATED EXPOSURE

------------------------------------------------

The more times you expose yourself to material, the more ingrained it becomes in your long-term memory. To make sure that you remember something, look at and think about it repeatedly over a long period of time. You are much better off studying a list of key terms for an hour each day for five days than studying it for five hours on one day. By looking at the list every day, you train yourself to retrieve that information from your memory after some time has passed. You will find that you get better at remembering information as the week passes, and you will begin to retrieve the information from your memory faster and with less effort. In this way, learning becomes a habit.

# SLEEP ON IT

Believe it or not, studying right before you go to sleep can make it easier to recall that information later. Studies have shown that you are very likely to remember something that you read just before you go to sleep. While you are asleep, your mind processes the information, moving it into your long-term memory. There's no guarantee that studying just before bed will be more effective than studying at other times, but it is certainly worth trying.

Try reading over your review sheets or flash cards right before you go to sleep, and when you wake up the next morning, quiz yourself to see how much you remember. At the very least, studying the list each night for several nights before an exam allows you to expose yourself to the material repeatedly throughout your study period. And if that fails, you can certainly try putting your flash cards under your pillow and maybe, through osmosis or luck, their contents will seep through the pillow and into your mind while you sleep! But don't count on this study tip to have a 100 percent success rate!

# LAST-MINUTE CRAMMING

Sometimes, no matter how hard you study, you will find that certain terms are extremely difficult to memorize. When all other methods fail, you can create a last-minute cram sheet. The night before an exam, take a single index card and write down any terms, facts, phrases, or formulas you can't remember, along with very brief definitions or explanations. Be sure to include any difficult terms that are likely to show up on an exam. Photocopy or scan the final version of your cram card and place a copy in a side pocket of your backpack. Take this card to the exam and arrive at the exam room a few minutes early so you can study the card before the exam begins. (You can sit at a desk in the exam room and study the card if this is allowed; otherwise, you can find a place to sit outside the room.) Continue to look at the card until you are asked to put away your notes.

As soon as you receive your copy of the exam, write down everything you remember from the card in the margins of the examination booklet. Don't even look at a single question before you do this! Since you will have just looked at the card, the information should still be in your short-term memory, which means it should be easy for you to recall. You should be able to remember most of the information for at least five minutes. The cram card is a particularly effective tool for math and science exams. You can write the formulas on the card and read them over right before the exam. At the start, you can then write the formulas somewhere in the exam book and refer back to them. This way, you won't have to struggle to remember them every time you have to answer a question.

## DON'T BE AFRAID TO GET EXTRA HELP

If you need assistance in a class, first seek help directly from the teacher by going to his office hours or staying before or after class to ask questions. Make sure to do this in courses that are cumulative in nature (such as math), which means the content of the course builds on a foundation of work done previously in the class. If you don't understand the basic fundamentals, then the homework, quizzes, and tests that build on each other can become too overwhelming for you and will often result in a decline in your grades.

Having your teacher on your side is a benefit. If he knows you are trying hard and seeking extra help from him, then your effort will, in some small way, be recognized in your grade at the end of the term. Again, remember that part of your grade earned on your report card is usually subjective. How well does your teacher know you and recognize the effort you put into his class? The relationship that you create with your teacher is important. The same goes for your TA (if you have any grades doled out by graduate students or upperclassmen who are TAs for your class).

## THINK ABOUT HIRING A TUTOR

If you are in high school and find a subject particularly challenging, don't be embarrassed or afraid to ask your parents or classmates to help you find a tutor. Many students—both in honors and regular track—receive tutoring outside of class to reinforce and clarify what is being taught. Upperclassmen who have already taken the course can also serve as great mentors or peer tutors. Also, many colleges and schools offer tutoring services through their academic support centers. You can be matched up with an upperclassmen or graduate student who will assist you in the subjects in which you need help most.

If you've tried those options and they aren't available or don't help, consider hiring someone to help. Professional tutors can be expensive, especially when you (as opposed to your parents) are paying for them. See if you can barter with your tutor if you cannot afford one. For example, if you have a knack for building websites or can get a potential tutor a discount at a store where you might work, see if the person will consider swapping services or discounts.

A tutor can help reinforce what you are learning in class and clarify work or reading assignments that you may have misunderstood or never understood before. The stigma of having a tutor has waned over the years, and students often speak freely about the extra help they get. Tutors can also motivate you, help you with organization and study skills, and serve as an objective third party to your parents or teachers with regard to what is going on in class. A tutor can become a cheerleader and confidante as well. One-on-one attention can lead to great results. Just be sure you study together more than you socialize!

## READ OVER ALL YOUR NOTES

To begin studying for an upcoming exam, gather together all your notes from the course in one binder. This should not be a problem, since you've been putting your notes in a binder at home throughout the semester. Just be certain that you now have them all in one place, in a logical order.

The first step is to read these notes from start to finish. It is extremely important that you do this in one sitting, *without interruption*. You'll need several hours to finish. Reading them all in one sitting will help you concentrate more intently on the material; more importantly, it will allow you to develop a clear mental image of the course material as a whole. Rather than studying various bits and pieces of information related to the subject, you'll now be able to see how everything fits together as part of the overall course. Don't study several subjects at once, though, or one subject right after another. If you study several courses within a short period of time, the material can easily become mixed up in your mind, making it more difficult for you to remember specific details. Make sure you take a break of at least one hour before sitting down to read notes from another course.

# MAKE A STUDY SCHEDULE

When planning your study schedule, you need to think about the number of exams you are going to take and the amount of time you have available before each one. If you are preparing for only one exam and you have plenty of time to study, you can be flexible in your schedule. If you are studying for several exams in a brief time period, however, you need to create a strict schedule for yourself and devote certain hours each day to the study of specific subjects. In general, you should avoid studying too many weeks in advance; you want the material you've studied to remain fresh in your mind during the exam. At the same time, you need enough time to go over your notes, to prepare and work with master lists of themes and topics, and to read additional sources and perhaps get extra help.

To provide enough time to accomplish all this, you should begin studying about *five to seven days* before the examination. Remember, if you are studying for more than one examination, be certain to study only one subject at a time, and give yourself a break of at least one hour before beginning to work on another; otherwise, the material can easily become mixed together in your mind. Create a study schedule that divides your day into different study sessions and breaks. Each study session should be devoted to preparing for a single examination.

## YOUR WELL-BEING MATTERS

During the week prior to a major examination, it is extremely important that you get plenty of sleep instead of staying up late. You are doing some hard work, so allow yourself to take a rest sometimes. You may feel like you are getting a great deal accomplished by staying up late every night, but you are actually doing more harm than good. When you are overly tired, it is extremely difficult to retrieve information from your long-term memory. If you arrive at an exam feeling exhausted, you won't be able to work through problems with a clear head. The night before a major exam, you should give yourself a break and take it easy. That doesn't mean you should take the *whole* night off, though. Read over your study materials one last time to keep all of the information fresh in your mind, then watch TV or go to a movie. And make sure you get a good night's sleep.

# A STEP-BY-STEP STUDY PLAN

Here are some lists to help you plan out your exam preparation.

## Before You Begin Studying (Before Classes End)
» Get information from the professor on exam content and format.
» Try to get sample tests, if available.
» Find out the date, time, and location of the exam.
» Consider joining a study group with other hard-working and intelligent students.

## Five to Seven Days Prior to Exam
» Read through all your notes from classroom lectures and reading assignments.
» Create review sheets for each of your final exams.

## Two to Five Days Prior to Exam
» Quiz yourself on each review sheet for each subject multiple times.
» Work with note cards and use other memorization techniques to learn key terms.
» Take notes on general themes and think about possible essay questions.
» See the professor to ask last-minute questions if you have any.
» Meet with study group or partners, if you opt to do this.
» Read other sources, if time allows.
» Make sure you know where to go for the exam. Confirm the day, time, and location. If you are unfamiliar with the test site, go before the test day so you can see exactly where it is and how much time it takes to get there.

## The Night Before the Exam

» Conduct one final read-through of review sheets.

» Make a cram sheet of terms you still can't retain.

» Relax: see a movie or watch TV.

» Gather items to bring to the exam: pens (that work), a watch (that works), candy, gum, a drink, your final cram sheet, and other materials you may need (a calculator, books, etc.).

» Get a good night's sleep.

» Set two alarms before going to sleep!

## The Day of the Exam

» Think about some key terms for a mental warm-up.

» Eat a balanced meal with some protein (like eggs) the day of the test. A meal with lots of carbohydrates might feel like good comfort food, but if you eat too many carbs right before the test, the carbs will turn to sugars that can make you "crash" and be less alert during the test. Instead, opt for your comfort food the day *before* (or after) the exam.

» Stay hydrated, but not so hydrated that you have to leave the test to use the bathroom constantly!

» If you have an afternoon or evening exam, use the morning for a final read-through of your master lists.

» Remember to bring everything that you gathered together the night before the exam.

» Get to the exam site early to choose a good seat.

# DO YOU WANT A STUDY GROUP?

In preparing for tests and exams, you might decide to form a study group or work with a partner. This format for studying, however, is not for everyone. Before deciding whether or not a study group would help you, consider these advantages and disadvantages.

### Advantages of a Study Group

» When you get together with other students, you have the opportunity to learn from one another. One classmate, for example, may have better notes or a better grasp of a particular subject than you do. You can use her as a source of information to flesh out certain points in your own notes.

» Answering questions from your fellow students will help you study. Talking about a particular topic is an excellent way to gain familiarity with the material. In the process of describing and explaining a concept to someone else, you develop a better understanding of it yourself.

» Being part of a study group ensures that you study a certain amount of time before an exam; the group keeps you on a set study schedule. If you have difficulty motivating yourself to study, being part of a study group can give you the jump-start and structure you need.

» Being part of a study group provides emotional support during a difficult time. Studying for and taking exams can be an extremely stressful, emotionally draining experience, especially if you feel alone. Meeting regularly with friends going through the same experience can make you feel better. These meetings alleviate tension as you laugh with your friends and help one another through tough times.

## Disadvantages of Study Groups

» If the students in your study group have poor notes and don't really understand the subject matter themselves, you might spend all your time helping them and not receiving any help in return. You need to watch out for "moochers" who haven't done any work all year and merely want to copy your notes.

» Panicky students are a serious problem in a study group. There may be members who are so stressed out that, instead of providing emotional support, they make you more nervous about an exam than you were before. Additionally, the bulk of the study group's time may be spent trying to calm this one person down or discussing only the concepts he doesn't understand.

» Study groups often don't use time efficiently. You may spend several hours with a study group and find you've covered only a small portion of the material, much less than you could have covered on your own.

» Whenever a group of students gets together, there is going to be a certain amount of chatting, joking, and socializing. A large portion of time might be spent discussing some point you already understand; that's obviously not the best use of your time.

If you find your study group or partner is becoming more of a social group or a distraction from your studies, find another group or study alone. While your intentions may be good in partnering with others, sometimes, getting out of a group that is really not helping you improve as a student is a better choice to make. Choosing the right people for your study group is a way to avoid some of these major disadvantages. A good study group involves hard work and contribution from all members; everyone should be willing to work and should have something valuable to contribute to the group. It's also a good idea to limit the size of the group—a group with any more than five members will probably waste more time and be more trouble than it's worth. At the same time, if you think that you work better on your own, don't feel that you are at a disadvantage. Being in a study group does not guarantee study success.

# ATTEND REVIEW SESSIONS

Professors occasionally organize formal review sessions prior to an examination, where they are available to answer questions regarding course material. You should always attend these study sessions, even if you don't have a specific question. You never know what hints a professor might share about what will be on the test. It's also helpful to hear the professor (or TA) describe the major concepts and key terms again. Try to remember some of their phrases and terminology and use them in your exam responses. Prepare thoughtful questions for your review session. Be an active listener and seek clues in what your professor presents that may help indicate what will be on the upcoming exam.

Be cautioned, though, that these sessions tend to attract panicky students who use the time to voice their own fears and anxieties about the exam. In addition to wasting time in the session, these students can also make you feel stressed out. Do your best to ignore them. The only person you need to listen to at the review session is the professor or TA. Another problem that might arise is that one or two students will dominate the entire session with their questions. If you have a question, ask it right at the beginning to guarantee a response.

# READ AND REVIEW OTHER SOURCES

Consulting with and reading additional sources is a valuable study technique in the days prior to an examination. If you have additional time during your study preparation period, read a few outside sources, especially ones about concepts that you have trouble understanding. As you go over your notes and prepare review sheets, you may come across terms or ideas that you still don't understand.

You also may find that, as time passes, you forget important information. If so, turn to reliable online sources, test prep books (available by subject at a local bookstore), or the library for more information. Many academic encyclopedias and dictionaries, for example, might include listings for the key terms you've studied in class. By consulting these sources, you can find clear and concise explanations of these points. Use your computer to look up sources or seek the assistance of a librarian at your school or local library.

Even if you are not confused about a particular point, it's sometimes a good idea to read some additional sources. The more material you read, the more information you receive. And by reading about a subject in depth just before an exam, you immerse yourself in the material; you then enter the examination focused and comfortable with that subject.

# STUDY AIDES: USE THEM CAUTIOUSLY

Study aides such as CliffsNotes or SparkNotes can be great tools if used properly. However, be sure to use them as a supplement, not as a replacement, for reading a primary source. Consult them when the original text confuses you or you think you missed a significant theme or concept.

Teachers and professors are familiar with study aides sold in stores (such as CliffsNotes, SparkNotes, or lecture notes) and often avoid testing on areas that these study aides cover in great detail. Be sure you are familiar with your text as a whole, not just the highlights reviewed in a study supplement. Also, study guides on different subjects specifically written for high school or college students can be useful study aides. Just be certain that you use these guides only to supplement your own notes, not to take the place of them.

# TALK TO THE PROFESSOR ABOUT UPCOMING EXAMS

The most obvious source for information about an exam is the professor. After all, he is the one who makes up the test questions. Most professors take a few minutes during a class to explain the format of each test and the material to be covered. If an exam is approaching and the professor has not made such an announcement, take the initiative and ask.

Although you can inquire in class, talking to the professor after class or during office hours is, in some ways, more effective. The professor will be more inclined to talk with you at length when the chat is not taking up other students' time. You'll be able to ask more questions, and, if you're lucky, the professor might offer you more detailed information about the exam than he would have offered in class. These are some basic questions you can ask a professor about an upcoming exam:

» What is the format of the exam? Will there be short-answer questions? Multiple-choice questions? Essay questions? A combination of different types of questions?
» How many sections will there be on the exam? How many points will each section be worth?
» What percentage of your overall grade will the exam determine?
» What material from class will the exam cover?
» If the exam is a final, will the exam be cumulative (meaning it covers the entire semester's worth of material)? Or will it only cover a portion of the course material?
» Do you have any suggestions on how to study for the exam?

Try to see the professor at least one week before a scheduled exam; that gives you enough time to plan your study schedule accordingly.

# LOOK OVER OLD EXAMS

You can often get a highly accurate sense of what an upcoming exam will be like by looking at previous exams. In addition to providing examples of the kinds of questions likely to be included, they can be used for practice runs to test yourself on the course material. Some departments keep exams on file so that students can use them as study resources.

You can also try to find someone who has already taken the course and is willing to lend his old exams to you (if he still has them). Just be certain that you are not doing anything unethical by looking at old examinations. If the professor has given a graded exam back to the students, then she knows it is available for anyone to examine. On the other hand, if the professor collects the exams and does not return them, then she doesn't intend for them to be distributed among students. If you somehow get a "pirated" copy of an exam, you are committing a serious breach of ethics that can get you in big trouble. When you consider the penalties, you'll realize that it's just not worth the risk. But if the professor does allow it, try to find one of his old exams. This will provide you with the most accurate picture of your upcoming test.

# LISTEN FOR HINTS ABOUT EXAM CONTENT

Throughout the semester, be sure to listen for any clues about what might be on an exam. Clues can pop up anytime, so be on the lookout.

A professor might say, in a completely casual manner, that a particular concept or term is likely to show up on the exam. Or after making a certain point, a teacher might say something like, "If I were to ask a question on an exam about this topic, I'd ask you . . ."

Whenever your professor makes any reference to an exam, even in an off-hand manner, be certain you take note of it. In addition to blatant clues, the professor will probably give you subtle ones. Exam questions generally reflect the professor's personal interests and biases. Even if the course is a basic survey course, there will be some topics your teacher feels are important for you to know and are therefore more likely to show up on an exam than others. Anything your professor seems particularly serious or passionate about is a likely candidate for inclusion. Any point your professor makes repeatedly, or gives special attention to, is also likely to be the subject of a test question. Highlight these points in your notes to remind yourself to study them.

## CRAM CAREFULLY

The most effective way to study for an exam is to take several days, ideally a week, to prepare. Of course, not everyone is able to do that all the time. If you find yourself having to cram the day or night before a major test, do it wisely. The worst thing you can do is to pull an "all-nighter," drinking loads of caffeine or Red Bull to keep you awake. Even if you cover a great deal of material in those hours, you'll be so exhausted the next day you won't have the stamina to make it through the exam. You may know the material, but you won't have the energy to write a detailed essay, and your mind will be so foggy that you won't be able to remember what you did study.

You can cram (see previous), but make sure that you get enough hours of sleep to function and be alert. If you haven't taken detailed notes from classroom lectures and reading assignments all semester, then you have a problem. It is extremely difficult at the last minute to catch up on all that material. Whatever happens, don't get into this situation. No amount of cramming can make up for it.

# HOW TO SKIM A TEXT

If there's time to prepare for your test, skim as many readings as possible. In order to skim a text, read some or all of the following elements:

» Introductions and conclusions
» Summary paragraphs
» Chapter titles and subtitles
» Any words or phrases that are bold, italicized, or underlined
» Captions for diagrams and photographs
» First and last lines of all paragraphs

As you skim, if a particular word, phrase, or line catches your attention and seems significant, consider reading the entire paragraph. Cramming and rushing through readings are not ideal ways to feel ready for any academic challenge. In fact, once you have been through the experience of cramming and skimming texts, you may find that the anxiety you experience while trying to catch up on a semester or entire school year is just too stressful and not worth it. Remember how this feels the next time testing rolls around, and maybe you will find yourself becoming better prepared.

# FINISH THE MARATHON

You may think that passing an exam is solely a matter of how much of the course material you've memorized throughout the term. However, a final exam is somewhat similar to running a marathon. Even though most marathon runners run almost every day, they move their training into high gear during the weeks before a major race, running longer hours and farther distances so they will be ready for the upcoming event. Most high-level runners also work hardest during the final minutes of the run, pushing themselves to give their all and finish strong.

In a similar way, you should move your studying into high gear before a test by really focusing on the subject matter. The methods and strategies previously outlined will help you do that. You don't need to be a bookworm or genius to ace a test, but you do need to be an academic athlete, willing to train hard to achieve a winning grade on an upcoming exam.

# CONQUER STRESS AND PANIC

Regardless of how prepared (or ill prepared) you may be, preparing for and taking examinations can be stressful. This stress can become panic, which is a serious problem that plagues many students. Before an exam, anxiety can keep you from studying effectively; during an exam, it can make you fail. However, there are some helpful strategies for fighting panic. One important antidote is having a clear, well-thought-out plan of attack. Not having a plan is like going on a trip without a map—you worry about where you're going, and, before you know it, you get lost. Having a good test-taking strategy gives you more control of the situation and makes you more confident of your abilities.

# REMEMBER THE BIG PICTURE

One major cause of panic is the tendency to blow the significance of exams completely out of proportion, to think each exam is a matter of life or death. It's extremely important to put the exams into perspective by remembering the big picture. A single examination is only a small part of your overall educational experience and an even more minuscule part of your life. In future years, no one is ever going to ask how you did on a specific exam in school. You probably won't even remember the test yourself. Bombing one will not scar you forever. Learn from your mistakes and do better next time. This way, you can move forward and recover from your setback.

Moreover, doing poorly on an examination is not a reflection of you as a person. It's not even an indication of intelligence. Some people are simply better at taking exams than others because they've developed successful test-taking skills—skills you can also learn. Doing poorly on one exam does not mean you'll do poorly on others. If you find that you continue to do badly, you should seek help. You can work regularly with a tutor and, most likely, improve your examination performance.

# AVOID ALARMISTS

No matter what, stay away from the alarmists. These are completely stressed-out students who try to pass their panic on to you. What is truly alarming is how successful they can be at shaking your own confidence. Once they approach you and convey their own fears, you'll find that you are starting to get nervous, too. Panic is infectious; before you know it, you'll be freaking out right alongside them.

Be especially wary of rumors. Chances are that what you hear about the level of difficulty of an upcoming examination or about specific questions is just scuttlebutt. If you let this sort of thing sidetrack you from your own study preparations, you'll be wasting time.

Avoid alarmists as much as possible, especially in the days before an exam. Many will get to the examination room early and ask fellow students to explain things they don't understand. If an alarmist corners you and asks how you feel about the test, politely tell her you are studying as best you can and don't want to worry about what is on the exam until you get there.

There's really no point explaining various terms to one of these people; this type of interaction only gets everyone into a nervous frenzy just as the teacher is passing out the examination. In fact, don't talk about the test or the material with other people. The last thing you need to worry about before an exam begins is how much of the subject someone else understands. Stay calm and focused, and be confident about what you've already studied. Don't let panicked classmates freak you out. If you have studied and know the material you are being tested on, try to block out others' panic and think for yourself. You can succeed despite their dire predictions! Don't let the fears of others bring you down.

# TAKE BREATHERS

Studying for and taking examinations is a physically and mentally exhausting procedure. It's crucial that you give yourself frequent breaks to help you relax. Don't study for more than two hours without taking a breather. Take a short walk, stretch your muscles. Even a ten- or fifteen-minute break can help you feel revived.

It's just as important that you take a breather while taking an examination. If you are not worried about the time, you can break in the middle of the exam by asking to be excused to get a drink or go to the bathroom. If you don't want to leave the room, you can take a breather right at your seat. Even if you don't do that, put your pen down and give your hands a short rest. Take your eyes off the exam booklet and look out the window or around the room; just make sure that you don't look anywhere near another person's paper, or you might be accused of cheating. Lift your arms in the air to stretch your back muscles and roll your head around to ease tension in your neck. Take several really deep breaths. A breather like this only needs to take about thirty seconds, but it will help you remain calm and focused.

# PRACTICE RELAXATION EXERCISES

Psychologists and therapists teach many relaxation techniques for coping with stress and panic. You can use these techniques while studying for exams and even while taking them. If you are particularly prone to stress, you may want to buy a book or audio guide that teaches relaxation exercises.

Try some visualization exercises. Here is one basic technique that you can start doing right away. Do this exercise a few times before an exam so that it will work more effectively during an actual test. As you practice it, you'll be able to experience that feeling of safety and happiness more and more quickly—in as little as thirty seconds—just by closing your eyes and breathing deeply.

Sit in a chair with a firm back and place your palms, face up, on your thighs. Close your eyes, and take deep breaths. Concentrate for a few seconds on your breathing, on the feeling of air going into and out of your lungs. Next, picture yourself somewhere you've been where you felt safe and happy. See yourself there. Use all your senses. Remember the sights, smells, and sounds of being there. Think about this scene for several moments, continuing to breathe deeply. Enjoy the feeling of safety and serenity you know while you are there. Sit for as long as you like in this place. When you are ready to leave, count to five, and then open your eyes.

# OTHER RELAXING ACTIVITIES

Try other ways to relax. Attend a yoga session or other relaxing exercise class offered at your school or local community center. Just following a trainer's instructions can assist you in centering yourself, refocusing, and calming your anxiety. Or, listen to music you like in a quiet place like your bedroom, or even in the privacy of your car. Focus on the different elements of the music, heightening your senses to the sounds that you hear. Keep your mind on the music and your breathing. Allow the song to soothe you. You could get a sound machine for your room or download songs that feature white noise, the sounds of nature, or running water. Keep these soothing sounds on to help you calm yourself when you feel stressed.

# CHAPTER 8
# SUMMARY

» Good studying needs to become a habit. Adopt an effective study routine for everything you do.

» Find a strategy that suits your learning style and stay consistent.

» Study in your room if you can create a space free from distractions and conducive to getting work done.

» Be careful not to fall asleep when you study. Practice many of the suggestions offered in this chapter to help you stay alert.

» Organization is a key component of academic success.

» Create a system of flash cards to assist you in memorizing.

» Try memory building exercises and strategies to improve your memory such as alliteration, mnemonics, and mental associations.

» Avoid last-minute cramming, but if you do, create a detailed cram card.

» Seek extra help when necessary to fully comprehend your teacher's expectations and content.

» Hire a tutor for extra support or to assist you in the coursework that most challenges you.

» Create a study schedule to keep you on task.

» Stay healthy and get plenty of sleep, especially during exam week.

» Follow the step-by-step study plan suggested in this chapter.

» Decide if a study group would benefit you.

» Always attend review sessions, even if you don't have a specific question. You never know what hints a professor might share about what will be on the test.

» Use study aides with caution; don't rely solely on them to act as a summary of your course.
» Talk to your professor! Attend office hours, ask questions, and listen to what he has to say.
» Look over old tests and exams to help you prepare.
» Try to manage your stress level and don't panic. Practice relaxation exercises.
» Take breaks.

- - - - - - - - - - - -

# ACE TESTS, QUIZZES, and FINAL EXAMS

The hour or two that you spend taking your quizzes, tests or examinations demonstrates to the teacher what you have learned, how you analyze and grasp the content of the class, and even how well your teacher has taught the material. Sometimes, your entire grade can come down to one test. Don't forget to breathe deeply and feel confident that you have done your best to prepare. This chapter focuses on final exams. You can modify every entry in this chapter to pertain to quizzes and tests as well. Quizzes and tests are just smaller versions of exams. The final exam is a cumulative experience involving the entire term, semester, or school year, while quizzes and tests focus on just a few weeks' worth of material.

# THE DAY OF THE EXAM

The most crucial thing to remember on the day of the exam is to set your alarm and give yourself enough time to get ready, especially if your exam is in the morning. More than one student has slept through a major test, and it's hard to get sympathy from the professor when this happens. If your alarm is unreliable, or if you have the habit of turning it off in your sleep or hitting the snooze button, then set several alarms, including ones on your cell phone, laptop, or watch. You may even want to arrange to have a friend or relative give you a back-up call.

In addition, get enough sleep *two* nights before your exam. Sometimes, a lack of sleep from a previous all-nighter hits you two mornings later, not the next morning. So, get your rest leading up to your test!

The morning of the exam, think about some key terms or general themes that will show up on the exam. This mental exercise gets your brain warmed up and focused on the subject matter. If your exam is in the afternoon or evening, you can read over your notes in the morning. But don't overburden yourself. A final read-through should be all you need to put you in the right frame of mind for the exam. Don't spend this time trying to memorize or learn new material. After this read-through, do something to take your mind off the exam, such as taking a walk or watching TV.

On the day of the test, eat a well-balanced meal with some protein to give your body an energy boost. Don't eat too large a meal, though— that will make you sleepy. Make certain you know exactly where the test is being given and leave yourself enough time to get there. Try to get to an exam about fifteen minutes before it is scheduled to start; this will ensure that you don't arrive late, flustered, and out of breath. You also want to have the benefit of using the entire time allotted for the exam, from the first minute to the last.

# BRING ALL OF YOUR MATERIALS AND CHOOSE A GOOD SEAT

Bring several blue or black pens, pencils, and a good watch. You might also want to bring some gum, candy, or a water bottle, if those are allowed. Make sure that your watch is working or that there is a clock in the room; it is crucial to keep track of time during the exam.

When you get to the test room, choose your seat carefully. You might, for example, want to sit near a window so that you can look up every so often and take a break. You could also sit where you can see the clock, if there is one in the room.

Before the exam begins, avoid talking about anything related to the test with other students, especially alarmists and "panickers" (see previous). You can sit at your desk and glance over your last-minute cram sheet, if you've made one. But don't get involved in a detailed question-and-answer session with other students; it's really too late to learn any major point. Moreover, if you listen to someone else, you risk becoming confused about something you were previously quite certain you understood. This last minute session will only serve to make you more anxious. Stay calm so that you can take the exam with a clear head.

# TEST-TAKING STRATEGIES

When you arrive to the testing room or exam site, try to remain as relaxed as possible. At this point, you either know the material or you don't, so hope that your preparation was sufficient and that there will not be too many surprises awaiting you.

When you get the exam sheet, don't just dive in and begin answering questions. Instead, take a moment to glance through the entire exam to see how it is structured and get a sense of the kinds of questions waiting for you. That way, you can devise a "plan of attack" that ensures that you use your time most efficiently. This preliminary read-through minimizes the tendency to panic midway into the exam. Look through the exam to see how many sections there are, the types of questions included, and how the point values for each section distribute. Then, create a rough mental schedule for yourself, allotting a certain amount of time for each section depending on how many points it is worth and its level of difficulty. Obviously, the more a section is worth, the more time you should devote to it. For example, if an hour-long exam is divided into a short-answer section worth fifty points and an essay portion worth fifty points, then you should spend an equal amount of time for each section, thirty minutes. If the short-answer section is worth only thirty points, however, and the essay portion is worth seventy, then you should spend much more time on the essay section. Take into account the levels of difficulty of each section. For example, if you find short-answer questions much easier than essays, you can allot additional time to the essay portion of the exam by getting the short answers done and out of the way.

The other advantage to looking at the entire exam beforehand is that you won't have any surprises waiting for you. It is extremely helpful, for example, to know if there is an essay section following the multiple-choice questions. That way, while you are answering the multiple-choice questions, you can also be thinking about how you will approach the essay. You might also come across short-answer questions that include terms or give you ideas for things to include in the essay!

# STRATEGIES FOR SHORT-ANSWER QUESTIONS

There are three types of short-answer questions that are commonly asked on examinations: fill-in-the-blank, true-or-false, and multiple-choice. Although there are different strategies for each type of question, you can follow the same general techniques to answer them. The following entries discuss these strategies.

# READ DIRECTIONS AND QUESTIONS CAREFULLY

Students often make the mistake of diving right into exam questions without reading the directions. The directions include important information you need to know *before* you start answering questions. You may, for example, not be expected to answer all questions on the exam, but will instead have a choice of which ones to answer. You won't know that, though, unless you read the instructions. It would be unfortunate to take the time to answer all fifty multiple-choice questions when the directions told you to choose only thirty. Or, the directions might also indicate whether you are penalized for incorrect answers. If you are penalized, then you won't want to guess as often.

In addition, you must read all of the questions thoroughly before answering them. Read the entire question and, if it is a multiple-choice question, look at all the possible choices as well. Don't read the first few words or skim the question and think you know the answer. Sometimes, the wording of a question (or the choices on a multiple-choice question) will look familiar to you for some reason so you'll assume you know the answer. However, when you read the question carefully, you may find that even if an answer sounds right, it could be wrong.

When students get short-answer questions wrong, it's often the fault of "trick words" they've overlooked. These are crucial words tucked into the question that completely determine the correct answer. Here is a list of trick words frequently found in exam questions: *not, always, sometimes, never, all, some, none, except, more,* and *less.* Always be on the lookout for these words; if you see one, underline it in the question so you can keep the word in mind as you attempt to determine the answer.

# PACE YOURSELF

Time is of the essence, especially on an exam. Therefore, you've got to watch the clock and pace yourself to be sure that you get to all the questions. When you first get the exam, look at the total number of questions and how much time you have to answer them. You can then figure out approximately how much time you have to answer each one (but keep in mind that you may spend more time on the harder questions and less time on the easy ones).

Check the time frequently. It's a good idea to get in the habit of checking your watch every time you turn the page of the exam. Monitor your progress and look at how many more questions you have to go. If you find you are going too slowly, then try to pick up the pace. In multiple-choice tests, if you choose to skip a question, circle the number of the question you skipped on both your test *and* answer sheet so that you remember to go back. Otherwise, you can be off by a number, which fouls up your entire test. Difficult questions will require more thought and time. When you get stuck on a particular question, you risk using up time that could be spent answering easier questions—the ones you immediately know, without a doubt. If you come across a very difficult question, skip it for the moment; that way you make sure that you will get to all the questions you can answer easily and, in turn, earn all of those points. After completing all of the easy questions, go back to the tricky questions and take the remaining time to work on them.

# GUESS INTELLIGENTLY

Chances are, you are not going to know the answer to every single question on an examination; on a fill-in-the-blank, true-or-false, or multiple-choice question, though, you can always guess. And, if you guess intelligently, you have a decent shot at getting the answer right.

Intelligent guessing means taking advantage of what you *do* know in order to try to figure out what you *don't*. It makes much more sense than random guessing. The next few entries give you techniques for intelligent guessing. Keep in mind, however, that guessing may not pay off on tests that penalize you for guessing.

## GUESSING ON FILL-IN-THE-BLANK QUESTIONS

Fill-in-the-blank questions are the most difficult to make guesses on because you usually need to supply the answer yourself—you aren't always given a selection of choices as you are on a multiple-choice question. Try to identify a general theme that the question reflects, and think about the key terms that relate to it. There's a strong chance that one of those terms will be the correct answer. You can also look for and underline the key terms within the statement and think about any related concepts you have learned in class.

## GUESSING ON TRUE-OR-FALSE QUESTIONS

It almost always pays off to guess on true-or-false questions because you have a fifty-fifty chance of getting them right. If you are uncertain about the answer, test the statement by finding specific cases that support or counter it. For example, if the statement asserts that a particular phenomenon is *always* true, you only need to think of a single case when that statement is not true and the answer will be false. Similarly, if the word *never* is included, you only need to think of a single case when the statement is true and the answer will be false. When you come up with specific cases that support your guess, you can be confident that your answer is correct.

# GUESSING ON MULTIPLE-CHOICE QUESTIONS

The key to guessing on multiple-choice questions is to eliminate as many of the choices as you can. With each elimination, you raise the odds of picking a correct response. If you can narrow down to two choices, then you've got a fifty-fifty chance of getting the question right—the same odds as on a true-or-false question.

There will usually be at least one choice you can eliminate right off the bat because it is obviously wrong. After that, examine each choice and see if there is anything incorrect within the answer itself. If the choice can't stand on its own as an accurate statement, then it is probably not a correct answer and you can eliminate it. For example, a possible choice might include a key term with the wrong definition. In that case, you know it won't be the right response.

Finally, you can eliminate choices that don't reflect the same general theme as the question. A choice that relates to a completely different theme most likely will not be the correct answer. Also many multiple-choice questions include the options "all of the above" and "none of the above." When these statements are included, it becomes much easier to make a guess. Look at the other choices. If you identify one that you think is an accurate answer, you can confidently eliminate the "none of the above" option. By the same token, if you are only allowed to include one answer, and you find two choices that are accurate answers, the "all of the above" option must be the correct answer.

Watch out for choices that are correct and accurate statements on their own; they aren't always the correct answer to the question. Just because a choice is itself an accurate statement doesn't mean it is correct in the context of the question. Once you narrow down the responses to two options, don't spend too much time pondering and evaluating which one is the right choice. Just go with your gut instinct; your first impressions are usually right. And once you've filled in your guess, don't go back and change it unless you later figure out the correct response with absolute certainty. Sometimes, for example, a later question will include information that sparks your memory or helps you figure out the answer to an earlier question. If that happens, go back and change the answer. Otherwise, forget about the question and forge ahead.

# TEST PENALTIES

On some examinations, you are penalized more for putting in an incorrect answer than you are for leaving the question blank. On those tests, it won't always pay off to guess. If you can narrow down your choices to two or three possibilities, however, it is usually advantageous to guess, since the odds are in your favor. If you have trouble understanding the question, read over it a few times to see if you can get at least the gist of it. Don't worry about specific words you don't know. Focus instead on what the question is essentially asking. Does it want you to:

» Supply a key term?
» Provide a definition of a term?
» Provide an example or illustration of some idea?
» Figure out the exception to some rule?

If you can grasp the nature of the question, you may be able to narrow down the possible answers. If there is a question that you simply do not understand, go to the professor, teacher, or proctor and ask about it. Chances are that some other classmates have similar questions, and, if enough of you ask, perhaps clarification will be given during the test time. If you never ask, you risk being penalized and not being able to make up for the error. Also, when you read over the question, underline any key terms. What general theme or topic is associated with those key terms? If you think more about that general theme, what related concepts or issues come to mind? Do any of these topics seem to tie into the question? If it is a multiple-choice question, look at the various choices. Do you understand them? Do any of them contain key terms that are familiar? Sometimes, even if you don't understand a specific question, you may be able to make a guess based on your overall knowledge of the general theme.

# VISUALIZATIONS

You might find, in the midst of an exam, that you've forgotten some piece of information that you know you've studied. This situation can be particularly frustrating because the answer is stuck somewhere in your long-term memory and you are having trouble accessing it. Close your eyes and try to picture the page from your notes on which the information is included. Try to "see" the page in your mind. Can you "read" the information on the page? Picture yourself studying those notes wherever you actually studied. Sometimes, by visualizing where you originally studied some piece of information, you can remember it. If none of that works, skip the question and move on to others. You may find that as you answer other questions, you will remember the information you needed for an earlier one. Memory is a mysterious mechanism; sometimes it resists pressure until you are distracted.

# ESSAY QUESTION STRATEGIES

Since you've brainstormed possible essay topics as you reviewed your notes, you will likely find that you are prepared for most of the essay questions on your exam. You can recall how you "talked through" possible essays and can write some responses using that framework. Here are some additional tips.

Read the questions carefully, and don't begin writing until you have read the questions in their entirety and are certain you understand them. Essay questions will not always be written in a straightforward manner, and you may have to think about what exactly the instructor is asking of you. Sometimes, for example, teachers write lengthy essay questions that include more information than the actual question, such as quotations or anecdotes. Or there may be several questions related to a common topic, all of which you need to address in your response. There are also essay questions that are not even phrased as questions, but tell you to discuss or address some topic. Read carefully and try to identify exactly what you need to cover in your essay. Underline any lines or phrases that specifically indicate points you should consider.

# CHOOSE YOUR ESSAY QUESTION

On many exams, rather than being given a single essay question, you will be given a choice of several. Choose carefully and select the question on which you can write the most impressive essay. For each one, consider your knowledge of the topic and the specific points you would present in an essay. You might even jot down a few notes next to each question, indicating your thoughts. Choose the question you have the most to say about and feel most confident answering. Don't waste too much time agonizing over the choices—that's time that you could spend actually writing. Look at the questions, think about each one, and make your decision.

Once you've made your decision, stick with it. Students sometimes lose their nerve halfway through their essay and decide to try answering a different question. By then, however, they have little time left, which makes it difficult—if not impossible—to write an adequate response. You are generally better off sticking with your first choice and doing the best you can; even if you get stuck midway, you've probably written more than you could write if you started on another question.

# CONFUSING OR DIFFICULT QUESTIONS

It's always possible that you'll get a complex essay question that doesn't tie neatly into a particular theme. The professor may be trying to challenge you—testing your ability to grapple, on the spot, with a very difficult topic.

Examine the question and think carefully again about what is being asked. Remember, no matter how confusing the question looks, it must tie in somehow with the subject matter. Remind yourself that because you've spent a great deal of time immersed in this subject, you are equipped to discuss it. Look for any key terms or phrases you understand, and think about corresponding general themes. You can sometimes discuss the general theme in a very broad sense and still get partial credit.

Whatever you do, make sure that you always write *something*. Worst-case scenario, write some kind of an answer and hope for partial credit. Try to write a confident, well-organized response based on course material, one that addresses something pertinent to the question. You'll show the professor you learned something, and this should earn you some credit.

# NEATNESS COUNTS—A LOT!

If your professor has to struggle to read your essay, he is not going to view it very positively, even if you've written a brilliant response. That's why, whether it's fair or not, neatness counts. Use a black or blue ink pen, but not one that smudges easily. Or, consider using a pencil. If you use a pen, write on only one side of a page in the exam booklet, since the ink can show through and make your response difficult to read. Most importantly, write as neatly and legibly as possible. If your hand-writing is difficult to read, then focus on writing more neatly. It may take you a little longer, but your response will be neater and, therefore, worth the time it takes.

As you are writing, you may find that you need to make changes; neatly and clearly cross out a line or a section or add additional infor-mation to a previous paragraph. Cross out a section by drawing a line through the material; don't scribble over or blot out what you've writ-ten. To add a line or passage, write in the top margin of the page, circle the passage, and draw an arrow down to the spot where it should be inserted. Using a pencil, however, eliminates these problems. When you finish writing, proofread your work. If necessary, add a caret symbol (^) to insert an extra idea that comes to mind after you review your work. Sometimes, having a clearer head helps you remember other points or ideas.

# COMMUNICATION IS KEY IN YOUR ESSAY QUESTION

As you write your essay question, remind yourself that you are writing for a specific audience (your professor) with a specific purpose in mind (to communicate how much you have learned about the subject). You want to make it crystal clear that you not only learned the material of the course, but you mastered it. That confident attitude should be reflected in the content and style of the essay.

Adopt a tone that indicates your attitude toward the material. Use sophisticated vocabulary and terminology, but not in a forced or incorrect manner. Include as many relevant key terms as possible, along with explanations and definitions. You may even want to underline the key terms, so that they will stand out even if the professor skims the essay. Feel free to be a "name-dropper" and cite other sources you may have read. Include as much relevant information as you can that will communicate the breadth of your knowledge and learning. Be careful as you communicate your thoughts in an essay. Don't, under any circumstances, include anything that is incorrect or that you don't fully understand. If you include any incorrect information, it will make a very poor impression and the professor may penalize you severely, even if other points are correct. You are better off leaving out a particular term or point altogether if your use of it is incorrect.

While you want to convey the breadth of your knowledge, you don't want to pad the essay with irrelevant facts. You can include some that are related, but not central, to the essay, but don't throw in everything but the proverbial kitchen sink. Don't bring up topics or terms that have nothing to do with the essay. If you do, the professor will think that you don't really understand the question. Include only the points you know are relevant and that will impress the professor.

# THREE-PART ESSAY STRUCTURE

On an exam, you don't have much time to plan a detailed, complex structure. You can use the standard three-part structure—similar to what you would use for a five-paragraph essay—that includes an introduction, body, and conclusion. This format particularly lends itself to examination questions because it provides a rigid structure. You don't have to think about the organization; you merely plug the relevant information into those three parts.

» **Introduction.** If the introduction is clear and intelligent, the professor will gain a favorable impression that will remain with him as he continues to read. It only needs to be a single, short paragraph in which you establish the general topic of the essay. The simplest way to do this is to write a few sentences that essentially rephrase and expand on the question. You should also include a thesis statement that summarizes the central issue of the question.

» **Body.** Be certain you divide the body into organized paragraphs, each centering on a specific point that supports the overall topic of the essay. If you've taken a few moments before you started writing to jot down your ideas and plan the order in which you will present them, you should be able to write an organized body without too much trouble. It's usually more effective in an exam to include many short paragraphs rather than a few long ones, since it appears you are raising many different points.

» **Conclusion.** On an exam essay, the conclusion is as important as the introduction. Some professors only skim essays, especially if they have many to grade, but they usually read the introduction and the conclusion, so use these parts to your advantage. The conclusion is the final impression your professor gets, and it comes right before he gives your essay a grade. You don't need to have an especially provocative or creative conclusion; you only need to summarize the key points within the essay. This will show the professor that you have successfully answered the question and know the subject matter. The conclusion doesn't have to be especially long, either—a few sentences will do.

# WATCH THE TIME

Check the time frequently to be certain you have enough time to get all the way through the essay. It's easy to get caught up in a single point, only to find time is running out and you have to rush through the rest of the response. Pace yourself and move quickly by allotting a certain amount of time to address each point and sticking to the schedule. If you are running out of time, finish whatever point you are on and jump ahead to the conclusion.

Make sure that you include a conclusion, even if it is just a few sentences. In the summation, you might refer to some of the additional points you would have made if you had had more time. This will let the professor know that you are aware of the information. If you have so little time that you can't complete the essay or write a conclusion, make a brief outline listing the points you planned to address. The professor will see that you do know something about the subject and might give you partial credit. Include a brief note apologizing for not completing the essay because of lack of time. You might get some points for doing this—and every point counts.

# AFTER THE EXAM

Exams can give you valuable insights into your strengths and weaknesses as a test-taker. Examine your tests after they've been graded. If the exam was given during the school semester, your professor will probably give it back to you. If the exam was a final, you may need to make an appointment with the professor and ask to see it. Your finals are especially important in preparing your strategy and course selection for your next semester.

When you get the exam, look through it and study any errors you've made. First, make certain you understand why you lost points. It's particularly important that you do this if later examinations in the semester will cover some of the same material. If you don't get these points right the first time, you're not going to get them right on the final unless you learn from your mistakes.

You can also talk to your professor about the exam. Ask for advice about what you might do in the future to raise your grade. This conversation is especially important if you have failed the exam. By doing this, you demonstrate that you are not a lazy or uncaring student and that you take the course seriously. With luck, the professor might offer valuable advice on how to study that will help you on future tests.

Sometimes teachers make mistakes when they grade exams. If you catch an error, think first about whether it's worth pointing out to the professor. Since you can create an unfavorable impression by drawing attention to the error, it's generally not worth quibbling over a few points. On the other hand, if a serious error was made in grading your exam, by all means point it out. Remember that in larger classes, professors don't necessarily do the grading themselves but assign it to a TA. So if their assistant made an error, they'll want to know about it.

If you did poorly or failed, don't get too down about it. Remember this one exam is a small part of a much bigger picture. Try, as much as you can, to turn it into a learning experience; even if you fail a test, you gain some knowledge that can help you in the future.

# CHAPTER 9

# SUMMARY

» Get enough sleep, wake up on time, and (if there is time) plan a light review the day of the exam.
» Be sure you have all of the materials you need with you at your exam (e.g., number two pencils, a calculator, water bottle, etc.).
» Select a good seat in your exam.
» Try one of several test-taking strategies outlined in this chapter.
» Read the directions carefully so you know what is being asked of you.
» Watch the clock and pace yourself to be sure that you get to all the questions on your exam.
» Practice intelligent guessing techniques on fill-in-the-blanks, true-or-false, and multiple-choice.
» Be aware of the test penalties (for guessing) on your exam. They differ from class to class.
» Visualizations can help if you forget something during a test.
» Read carefully and try to identify exactly what you need to cover in any test with essays. Underline any lines or phrases that specifically indicate points you should consider.
» When offered a choice of essay questions for a test, look at the questions, think about each one, and make your decision. Once you've made your decision, stick with it.
» Make sure your responses are legible and neat!
» In your essay, make it crystal clear that you not only learned the material of the course, but you mastered it.
» Try a three-part essay structure on your exam: introduction, body, conclusion.
» Pace yourself throughout your exam and essay writing.

# EXCEL BEYOND THE CLASSROOM

While the transcript is undeniably the most important component of your college application, being just a student is not your entire job. You need to find other activities to participate in outside of class that do not include watching TV, playing video games, or surfing the Internet. So, what can you do? Pick one activity and do it well. Or participate in a few activities, but be sure you are doing more than just showing up. Join a club, sport, or organization and stick with it throughout school. Also, try to find time to get a job and volunteer during your time outside of school. Piece of cake, right?

# CLUBS, ATHLETICS, AND ORGANIZATIONS

Being a participant in clubs, athletics, and organizations reflects another side of who you are (some people refer to that quality as being "well-rounded"). Find a few activities you enjoy doing or one main activity that permeates through all you do (sometimes people refer to students with narrow interests as a "pointy"). These choices offer your teachers, college admission officers, and others a glimpse into what else is important in your life.

All colleges have activity sections in their applications that require you to complete lists, write descriptions, and note hours dedicated to how you spent your time after school, on weekends, and during the summer. Make sure you have some items to add! If you don't take on leadership responsibilities in a club, be a "worker bee." Raise your hand and volunteer to do anything necessary to help in the club. Write e-mail blasts, distribute flyers, or man a booth at an event—anything. Do something other than just showing up at weekly meetings. Plan to stay committed for the long term and build up your role and involvement as a worker bee or eventual leader. By getting more involved, you will also have more to write about when it comes time to apply to colleges.

Most colleges ask you to elaborate on an activity outside of school that excites you. A student who lists involvement in multiple clubs but cannot articulate anything tangible that she has done other than attend meetings is really not an effective or hands-on club member. Those students who demonstrate "depth and breadth" are viewed more favorably than those who simply attend weekly meetings. If it is not in your nature to lead, join and help out. Who knows? Over time you may become a club leader.

# START A CLUB

If you have an interest and your school does not have a club to support it, take the initiative and start a club yourself. It is easier than you think! If you find yourself wanting to lead a club, take it on and go for it. Here's what you'll need to do:

» Fill out an application form at school to get permission to start your club.
» Put together your plans and a proposal, name your club, and define its purpose or mission.
» Get a teacher to be the club advisor or supervisor and secure a location and regular meeting schedule.
» Raise and designate uses for funds, plan events, bring speakers in to speak to your group, recruit members, and set goals.
» Learn to promote through flyers, e-mail blasts, blogging, your school paper, or other campus outreach.
» Learn to delegate tasks to members of the club and try to identify friends or classmates who can lead with you. Find underclassmen who will get involved so the club continues successfully even after you graduate.

Here are some ideas for off-the-beaten-path clubs:

» Music Video Club
» Cooking Club
» Pop Culture Club
» Scrabble Club
» Lawn Bowling Club
» Senior Citizen Support Club
» Hiking Club

» Classical Music Club
» Pet Owners' Club
» Astronomy Club
» 4-H Club
» Harry Potter Club
» Star Wars Club

# GET A JOB

Wherever you live, whatever your family's income level, and however much money your parents give you, at some point in your high school or college career you need to get a job. Being employed teaches you the real value of money and how much time and work it takes to make money. A job holds you accountable for being somewhere on time and answering to a supervisor other than your teachers or parents.

Working also demonstrates to colleges and graduate schools that you are seeking out adult responsibilities and signifies a level of independence that you are creating for yourself. Having a job during high school, especially if you live in an affluent area, shows that you know what it is like to earn a dollar instead of taking handouts from your parents.

Don't rely on a job filing papers at your dad's office or answering phones at your mother's workplace. Instead, seek out "common jobs," such as bagging groceries, scooping ice cream, or making pizza. Babysitting is just fine, too. These types of jobs are ones you can easily get without your parent's assistance and help demonstrate initiative on your part. Employers can also write college or graduate school supplemental recommendations for you. They can attest to your character in a different way than a teacher can, citing your work ethic, responsibility, and demeanor at work.

# WORK WARNINGS

During summer vacation, you could/should plan to work full-time; however, during the school year, if the time committed to working a job hinders your academic performance in any way, work only on the weekends, if possible. The *amount* of time you work is not as important as the fact that you *are* working.

Find something that will build your character and, perhaps, introduce you to a world different from your own. Your time spent in the working world will put things into clearer perspective for you. You'll never look at a $5 bill the same way, once you realize what it takes to earn it! Also, going through the process of completing a job application, interviewing with a supervisor or boss, and working out a shift schedule on your own is an adult experience. If the workload gets out of hand, try to hone your time management skills. Take ownership of your job experience in finding transportation (walk, bike, bus, drive, car pool) and being on time.

# IDEAS FOR STUDENT JOBS

Coming up with jobs that you can do in high school can be challenging since you may feel too young or inexperienced to work. Here are some good ideas for high school jobs:

» Ice cream scooper
» Coffee shop worker

- » Water park or theme park ride attendant
- » Grocery clerk or bagger
- » Fast-food worker
- » Landscaper or lawn mower
- » Car wash attendant
- » Babysitter
- » Dog walker
- » Retail stocker
- » Shopping mall kiosk attendant
- » Restaurant host or waiter

Bad ideas for high school jobs are anything that looks as though you had your parents' help or connections in getting the job or anything that can be viewed as working for your parents.

# VOLUNTEERING IS IMPORTANT

While getting a paying job builds character and experience, so does giving your time away for free. Community service has become a buzz-phrase in the college and graduate school admission world, and admission officers *do* expect teens to have experience and awareness that comes from giving back to their communities.

The secret is this: volunteer work does not have to be a drag. Take something you already like to do and extend it into the area of community service.

» If you like the beach, get certified and volunteer hours as a lifeguard or volunteer to organize a beach cleanup.

» If you enjoy drama, volunteer at an after-school Boys & Girls Club or community center and teach kids drama games and improvisation.

» If you play a sport, volunteer to be a referee or help coach youngsters.

Try to find something you like to do and link it to your community service. That way, what might feel like a chore becomes fun. If you leave a volunteer job having enjoyed yourself, feeling good about what you did, and wanting to return again, the job is right for you. Always remember, keep an open mind when it comes to trying new things.

# GO BEYOND MINIMUM HOURS

Many schools offer a minimum number of hours a student needs to complete in order to graduate. Use this number as just that: a minimum. In order to demonstrate that you weren't just volunteering to go through the motions, work beyond the hours required by your school. If your school does not have a minimum or even a requirement, volunteer anyway. Not only does it feel good to give back, it is your duty to help your community in some way if you are blessed with good health, an education, and a life that affords you some luxuries.

# MAKE IT PERSONAL

Volunteer work can be of almost any kind and take place anywhere. Local hospitals, Boys & Girls Clubs, Special Olympics organizations, soup kitchens, schools, religious organizations, shelters, libraries, and nonprofit organizations welcome students to assist in their organizations. Often, it is as simple as completing an application and showing up. Working in hospitals or other medical settings may require fingerprinting or blood tests for infectious diseases, so keep that in mind when applying.

While joining a volunteer organization such as National Charity League (NCL) can be a wonderful way to volunteer with your parents, you should also find something that is your own volunteer experience. NCL and other similar groups offer wonderful volunteer opportunities, but do something without a parent so that you can experience something more individualized.

You get out of your volunteering experiences what you put in. If you are passionate, committed, and excited to participate in your tasks assigned, the work will not feel like a chore. Volunteering can take you into a world outside of your comfort zone, such as a homeless shelter or soup kitchen, or it can serve as an extension of an existing talent or passion you have. If you have an interest that does not have a volunteer organization linked to it, think about starting your own. If you like drama and theater, plan a summer camp or after-school drama class for youngsters in your own neighborhood. Make flyers, e-mail parents, give a presentation, and start your own program.

# VOLUNTEER DOS AND DON'TS

» **Do** volunteer to do something you enjoy and find meaningful.

» **Do** strive to make deep connections and commit yourself to the volunteer activity for an extended period of time to demonstrate depth of interest.

» **Do** seek out connections with the people you work with at your volunteer site (not only the recipients of your time, but your covolunteers and volunteer coordinator).

» **Do** keep a personal log of hours you have committed to each organization.

» **Do** work hard as a volunteer, since sometimes your volunteer job can turn into a paid job.

» **Do** work beyond the hours that are the minimum requirement of your school to demonstrate your longevity and sincere commitment to the organization.

» **Do** show up on time, ready to work, with respect and commitment.

» **Don't** volunteer somewhere simply because you think it looks good for college or graduate school.

» **Don't** disparage or belittle your covolunteers, the organization, or people you serve.

» **Don't** treat a volunteer job as unimportant just because you are not being paid for your time.

# SPEND SUMMERS WISELY

As soon as you graduate from eighth grade, you are a high school student in the eyes of colleges. That means that, beginning the summer after eighth grade, your summers "count" for future college applications.

Does that mean you can't hang out, relax a bit, and decompress after a busy year in school? No. It just means you do need to plan some activities for yourself to keep your summers filled and meaningful through high school and college. Going to the beach, playing video games, hanging out at the mall, and watching television are not great answers to the college application question: How did you spend your high school summers?

You can certainly go on a family trip or two, unwind, and hang out, but be sure to fill the remaining time with some significant experiences. Whether you are attending summer school, working at a coffee bar, learning to play a musical instrument or speak a foreign language, or participating in some other activity, make sure to take advantage of the extra free time you have in the summer. Begin to think about your upcoming summer in January of that year, so you can look into application requirements for certain activities or programs. Sometimes, teacher recommendation letters are required when you apply so plan ahead (remember those all-important teacher relationships!). The next entries give you some activities to consider when planning your summer.

# THE ACADEMIC SUMMER

Participate in summer school courses or programs on college campuses—either close to home or far away. You do not need to take these courses at a college where you are planning to apply; any campus is fine. See if the program offers high school or college credit as a result of your participation. Obtain an official transcript and have one sent to your high school counselor as well when the program is complete.

Explore in great depth a subject that interests you. For instance, if you like English literature, take a course on William Shakespeare. Or, alternatively, try exploring an interest you have never cultivated but want to develop (such as a foreign language, film, music, anthropology, architecture, or forensics).

Virtually all college campuses offer summer programs for high school students or current college students. If you want to obtain credit, you need to see if the course will be transferable to another high school or university. If credit does not matter and you want to learn for learning's sake, take a course with a pass/fail or credit/no credit option. You may also choose to audit a class so that you can enjoy listening and learning but do not have to stress about testing or writing papers for the class.

If you travel with family or friends in the summer, try to find ways to make your trips educational and even academic. Read books about the history of the place you are visiting and go to museums and historic sites.

# STUDYING ABROAD

There are many opportunities for students to travel to a foreign country during the summer. Through these programs, you can work on your language skills, learn a new language in an immersion program, or just embrace a different culture. Some students want to live with a family in another country so they can gain an insight into another culture first-hand. Others prefer living in a dormitory environment with other students from around the world. There are pros and cons to both experiences.

National organizations support overseas experiences, such as People to People Sports Ambassadors at *www.sportsambassadors.org*, LeadAmerica at *www.lead-america.org*, or American Field Service (AFS) at *www.afs.org*. Also, many college campuses have relationships with universities overseas whereby you can gain transferable college credit by studying at those institutions. Check with your school before you go.

# SUMMER COMMUNITY SERVICE

Spend your summer giving back. Programs around the globe offer you the opportunity to make a difference in the world by donating your time to help build houses and schools or support communities much less fortunate than your own. Find out what your local religious organization has planned for a summer volunteer outreach program and sign up.

If you do prefer hanging out at the beach, by all means go there and enjoy it, but consider organizing a beach cleanup so you can do some community service while there. Find things you enjoy and brainstorm ways you can delve deeper into community service during the summer months and capitalize on the free time you have when you are out of school.

# SUMMER ATHLETIC PROGRAMS

Your sports team will certainly require you to do some training or camp over the summer. If you are a varsity athlete, you will probably be required to practice or play in a summer league, which makes it harder to find time for other organized programs. Colleges do recognize the large time commitment required to participate in sports. If you can, pursue a new athletic endeavor or some other sports-related activities such as coaching, working as a referee, or teaching at a community center or summer camp sports program.

College campuses offer a variety of organized sports programs in the summer under the guidance of college athletes and coaches. If you are in college, you can work or volunteer as a coach, and if you are in high school you can enjoy learning from excellent college athletes and coaches. Summer club sports teams also play and practice as well as compete in tournaments around the country (and sometimes internationally). Furthermore, there are showcases that high school athletes also attend in summers where college scouts look to recruit.

# OTHER SUMMER ACTIVITIES

Seek out leadership programs that teach you fundamentals of leadership through group and team-building activities. You will attain skills such as public speaking and teamwork, and often times, you will hear from local leaders in your area who share their leadership stories. What if leadership doesn't suit you? Are you a dancer? Singer? Musician? Artist? Actor? Seek out a program that allows you to hone your craft. Again, college campuses, conservatories, local theaters and repertories, and high schools offer classes in acting, technical aspects of theater, and other creative arts. What if you have an obscure interest? Do you love airplanes? Then take some simulated flying lessons, volunteer at an airplane museum, or try to take a behind-the-scenes tour of your local airport to learn more about aviation. Like to cook? Sign up for some classes at a nearby culinary institute or try to intern for a chef at any local restaurant. Do you dare climb a mountain? Get close to nature? Push yourself to limits you never thought imaginable? Live and survive in the great outdoors? Try some adventurous travel: the sky's the limit!

# FIND AND PURSUE YOUR PASSION

Through your years of schooling, you gain exposure to a variety of subjects, teachers, and extracurricular activities. During the course of your job as a student, you may have discovered the classes or activities that make you most excited. Find the classes about which you are most passionate, and immerse yourself in them throughout your high school or college experience.

# APTITUDE AND PERSONALITY TESTS

What if you have not yet identified your passion? If you have not discovered your goals in life and feel either lost or overwhelmed by the thought of selecting a major or pursuing a career path, you may be a great candidate for finding some answers and direction by taking an aptitude or personality test.

The best known of these multiple-choice tests is the Myers-Briggs Type Indicator (MBTI), which offers a series of pointed questions. The answers are not right or wrong, but instead indicate to the analyzer where your potential career and personal interests lie. How you respond to each question helps determine your personal strengths and possible career or academic interests, and your responses may assist you in finding a career path or college major that is right for you.

There are other ways to take personality tests that are less formal than the MBTI. Search online for some reputable personality tests you can take to help identify skills and passions you have that can be linked to college majors, internships, or careers. Professional career or guidance counselors are trained to assist you in finding a path and direction to take to pursue your academic or career aspirations. Many schools have in-house guidance counselors or advisors, but you can seek out an independent professional if you need a more in-depth study of what passions you might pursue. These professionals will interview you and use your verbal responses to help formulate and identify majors or career paths that would be a good fit for your personality type and interests.

# BE AN EDUCATED EDUCATIONAL CONSUMER

When you're a student, especially at a big school, it's easy to feel like a small part of a very large system. As you plow through miles of red tape and deal with headache-inducing bureaucracy, you can feel like you have no control over your education and that your only option is to do what you are told. Don't forget, though, that without students, there wouldn't be any education system. You are a vital part of any educational institution and, as such, you have a right to make as many demands of the system as it makes of you. Your education is at stake, and you have the right to get the best one possible.

If you read consumer magazines and advice guides, you'll see references to becoming an educated consumer. This means that before you make a large purchase, you do some research to get the best deals. Similarly, you should become an educated consumer of education. Get your money's worth from your college.

Being an educated consumer starts first with choosing a school that's right for you. There are more than 3,500 colleges and universities out there, but only a handful will suit your interests and needs. Don't choose a school haphazardly, based on what other people tell you, or based on where you think you want to go. Visit Facebook or college blog posts to hear directly from current students. Also, read different campus student newspapers online to get a better sense of the culture and flavor of the student body.

# RESEARCH YOUR COLLEGE CHOICES

Most colleges are different than the glossy promotional brochures make them out to be. It's a good idea to visit the schools in person so you can see how things really are. The administrators and admission office will tell you one thing about a school, but students may tell you something else. Try to talk to students and ask about their perspectives. Some questions you should ask:

» Do they like the school?
» Do they feel they are getting a good education?
» Are they happy with the choice they made?

Look carefully at recent statistics about the school (also available online).

» How many people drop out before graduating?
» How long does it take most students to get a degree?
» What percentage goes on to find jobs within a year of graduating?
» What percentage of students continues on to graduate or professional schools?

If these statistics are poor, the school may not be providing its students with everything an educational institution should.

Take time to tour college campuses, especially if they are schools to which you will apply. It is important to see what your goal is in doing this "job" called high school. Any time you are traveling near a college campus, even if it is close to home, take a tour, visit the bookstore, and ask current students lots of questions to get a feel for the campus culture. Don't be shy!

Once you have selected a college and started classes there, you should continue to think of yourself as an educated consumer. Most schools have a tremendous range of offerings; there are many different courses as well as many different teachers. Both teachers and courses, though, can range in quality. It would really be a shame to spend money for college credits and end up in courses that do not excite or appeal to you.

Sometimes, a course won't be good because its content isn't something that interests you. More often than not, though, the deciding factor is the professor. A dynamic teacher can make the most mundane subject seem interesting. A poor teacher, however, can make the most fascinating subject a total bore. Before you select classes, do some research to be sure you'll get what you want.

# WHERE WILL YOU GO?

There are many different sources of information you can consult to find which college is best for you. Because the following sources do not all provide the same kind of information, you should consult several of them. The more information you have, the more well rounded the picture of the school will be.

There are hundreds of college guides on the market. Many guides simply list basic facts about the schools, such as the number of students, the student-to-teacher ratio, requirements to graduate, majors offered, and average SAT scores of those admitted; other guides are more subjective, trying to paint a portrait of life at the school and to elaborate on each school's strengths and weaknesses. Both kinds of books can be quite valuable, particularly in the early stages of your college search when you are identifying a range of schools that are right for you.

As you narrow down your choices, you can get more detailed information from other sources. All colleges and universities have their own websites. Visit these sites and get a variety of information about a school. Check out online course catalogs, campus clubs and organizations, school traditions, and the student online newspaper. There are also several online college guides, many provided by the same publishers as the college guide books you see in the bookstore. In addition, you can write or e-mail specific schools and request information. Keep in mind, however, that their brochures are designed to present the school in the best possible light. Essentially, school-produced booklets and publications are public relations pieces and advertisements. Still, the brochure will provide important basic information. Be sure to peruse the online course catalog, too.

Among the online sites you can check out, for school ratings and other information:

» *www.petersons.com*
» *www.fiskeguide.com*

» www.princetonreview.com/college-rankings.aspx
» www.collegeprowler.com
» www.mycollegeguide.org

# FRIENDS, RELATIVES, AND CAMPUS VISITS

Ask people what college they are currently attending and how they feel about their choice. Ask specific questions about assets and drawbacks. Keep in mind, though, that each person is different. What one person may have loved or hated about the school may not affect you the same way.

Be wary especially of the legacy trap—just because a close relative went to a particular school and loved it does not mean it's necessarily the best place for you. Consider your own interests and needs, and find a school that meets them.

Visiting a school is an excellent way to get a tremendous amount of information about it (see previous). You'll see the campus the way it really looks, not as it appears in the fancy brochure photos. Go on a campus tour and check out the admission office where there is often some kind of information session for students. Make sure that you talk to students; they will give you an accurate assessment of the school from the student's point of view. If possible, arrange to stay overnight in a dormitory (some schools make this experience available to applicants).

Of course, visiting schools is time-consuming and can be expensive; you should plan to visit only the schools you are seriously considering.

Keep a notebook to log your campus visits. Note cool facts, traditions, campus tour highlights, e-mail addresses of students you may have met, and names of special classes or professors you may have collected. You will refer back to these notes when it comes time to apply to college and even may use some of the content you gathered in your actual college application questions.

## MAKE THE MOST OF SCHOOL

Throughout this book you have leaned that it is important to be an active rather than a passive student. That not only applies to your specific study tasks, but to your entire attitude as a student. You can't sit back and place your education entirely in the hands of others. Teachers, books, and other educational resources can only do so much; ultimately, you must take control of your own education if it is going to have any value. In part, this means getting help when you need it.

There are many resources available to help you when you are having difficulty, including caring teachers and tutoring programs, but you've got to make the effort to seek them out. At the same time, you can supplement your education on your own. Schools today are rich in resources and opportunities that can provide you with an exceptional, well-rounded education, from study-abroad programs and career internships to high-tech study centers and libraries. But these opportunities are not going to come knocking on your door; you need to take active measures to find and use them.

If you make the most of your education, it will eventually mean much more to you than a diploma hanging on the wall; it will mean that you have done a successful job in charting your path towards a future that you created. The foundation that your education provides is more sturdy and stable if you have taken an active role in crafting and working at it. In the meantime, good luck and happy studying.

# CHAPTER 10
# SUMMARY

» Create a full life for yourself outside of the classroom. Join clubs, athletics, and organizations to reflect another side of who you are.

» How you choose to spend your time outside of the classroom demonstrates what is important to you.

» Start a club. Appoint yourself president!

» Get a job. Apply, interview, and gain employment. Work for others to show you can be accountable, responsible, and independent.

» Find a student job to gain experience in a field or just to improve your people skills.

» Volunteer and give back to your community. Consider taking something you already like to do and extend it to the area of community service.

» Spend your summers wisely. Keep your summers filled and meaningful throughout high school and college.

» Find and pursue your passion.

» Take an aptitude or personality test to see where your personal and career strengths lie.

» Educate yourself about colleges.

» Use time wisely when visiting college campuses. Your goal is to try to get a feel for the vibe of a campus, so dig deep, speak to students and read their testimonials.

» Be involved in managing your school life. Take advantage of resources offered.

# FINAL REMINDERS

» Develop productive study habits and make them a part of your daily routine. Change bad habits into good ones.

» Treat being a student like a job; be professional, serious, and organized.

» Set tasks for each day, week, and month.

» Manage your time carefully; create a schedule that gives you flexibility each week to fulfill new tasks.

» Make the right impression on your teacher. Take pride in your work.

» Be an educated consumer.

» Take control of your education and make the most of it.

# TAKING A STANDARDIZED TEST

Whether getting your driver's license or taking the SATs, each test you take is a rite of passage that you'll have to go through when you reach a certain age or experience level. There are proactive ways you can plan and tutors available to assist you if you feel overwhelmed or in need of extra support and guidance as you navigate these types of tests.

## Types of Standardized Tests

There are many types of tests that you will be required to take during your high school and college years. Most colleges require that applicants submit results from one or more standardized test as part of the admission process. Almost all colleges will now accept the results from the SAT Reasoning Test (formerly the Scholastic Aptitude Test or the Scholastic Assessment Test) or the American College Test (ACT), both of which include a writing section. Additionally, some colleges, including the University of California and many other highly selective universities, require some combination of SAT subject tests. Your high school may have internal or state-mandated standardized tests such as the STAR testing or Stanford 9 test.

Below are definitions of the national tests used in the college admission process followed by the college-level testing required for graduate school admissions. These are just general overviews to familiarize you with the names of the various testing agencies.

### PSAT and PLAN Tests

The Preliminary SAT (PSAT) is similar to the SAT Reasoning Test but shorter in length, which students usually take in tenth grade. The test is not always a great indicator of how you will do on the real SAT, though. The PSAT is also known as the National Merit Scholar Qualifying Test (NMSQT), which identifies National Merit Scholars based on the scores they receive on this test. The PSAT is not required for college admission and scores are not reported to colleges. It doesn't hurt to take it, though, as it is good preparation for the SAT. The National Assessment Program for Literacy and Numeracy (PLAN) test is the prequel to the ACT test. Students take the PLAN in tenth grade. Some schools administer a test called EXPLORE (the pre-PLAN) in eighth or ninth grade.

### SAT Reasoning Test

The SAT Reasoning Test (formerly known as the SAT I) is a three-hour, primarily multiple-choice test, which measures verbal and mathematical reasoning abilities that develop over time. There is an essay-writing section as well. The test scale goes to 800 with math, verbal, and essay components, making the perfect score on this test 2400 points. The

SAT Reasoning Test and SAT subject tests are products owned by the College Board. Visit *www.collegeboard.com* for additional information.

### *ACT*

The American College Test (ACT) tests students in fours areas: English, mathematics, reading, and science reasoning. There is also an ACT Plus Writing test that has the previous four sections plus a thirty-minute writing section. Check to see if your colleges require the writing test (most colleges do). Also, most colleges will accept results of the ACT as an alternative to the SAT and, in some cases, the SAT subject tests. Here is a statement from the ACT.org website: "ACT results are accepted by all 4-year colleges and universities in the U.S. The ACT includes 215 multiple-choice questions and takes approximately 3 hours and 30 minutes to complete, including a short break (or just over four hours if you are taking the ACT Plus Writing). Actual testing time is two hours and fifty-five minutes plus thirty for the writing section (ACT Plus Writing)." The test is scored on a scale of one to thirty-six.

## Advanced Placement Tests

Advanced Placement (AP) exams are graded on a scale one to five. They are usually taken in May or June or after the completion of a specific AP course. Usually, a score of four or five will earn a student college-level credit, although that practice varies from school to school. A score of three will often assist with college placement in more advanced-level college classes (e.g., language placement, English, etc.) but a score of one or two on the AP exam generally won't.

### SAT Subject Tests

The SAT Subject Tests (formerly SAT II) measure a student's knowledge of particular subjects and his ability to apply that knowledge. A generation ago, these tests were known as achievement tests. The scale is the same range as the SAT (200–800). SAT Subject Test scores assist colleges with placement level of students in various courses. The tests also measure how well a student's school does in teaching subject material and how good of a multiple-choice test taker the student is. Students can take up to three subject tests in one day since each test is multiple-choice and an hour in length. (Visit *www.collegeboard.com* for a complete listing of subjects offered and current testing dates.)

## Which Tests Should You Take?

Students usually register to take either the SAT Reasoning Test and/ or the ACT in the spring of junior year. (Some choose to take it the fall of senior year since they feel less busy and overwhelmed by school-year commitments and can prepare the summer leading up to the test date.) Students have the option of taking either the SAT Reasoning Test or the ACT because colleges that accept both tests use a "conversion chart" to compare the scores. The higher score is used for admission purposes. In fact, some colleges will actually use the best combination of scores from various sittings of the tests in making an admission decision. There are even over 800 colleges today that have made the SAT or ACT optional for admission! You can see a list of these schools at *www .fairtest.org*.

All SAT Subject Tests should be taken as soon as you can after your completion of the course, so ideally in May or June (unless it is a one-semester class). You may already be studying for your exams or AP testing at the same time, so the material is no different. Check to see which math level your college will accept. Many do not count the Math Level 1C, for example. On each test day, a student can take either the SAT Reasoning Test *or* up to three SAT Subject Tests. Ideally, you should complete testing by December of your senior year or sooner if you plan to apply to some colleges earlier.

## Preparing for Standardized Tests

A good starting point in preparing for standardized tests is to read through the online sites and sample test booklets provided by the SAT and the ACT, which are available at your college counseling center at your school. Also, practice tests are offered on the websites. Test prep books are sold at bookstores or online, so they can be a good resource as well. Many tutoring companies offer preparation courses to familiarize you with the contents and assist in preparatory planning. The best preparation, though, is to take actual practice tests. Scores often improve dramatically because you have learned by experience how to take the test.

# RESOURCES

## High School

Gottesman, Greg. *College Survival: Get the Real Scoop on College Life from Students Across the Country,* 7th edition (New York, NY: Peterson's, 2004).

Gottesman, Greg. *High School Survival: A Crash Course for Students by Students* (New York, NY: Arco Books, 1999).

Riera, Michael. *Surviving High School* (Berkeley, CA: Celestial Arts, 1997).

## The Admission Process

Fetter, Jean. *Questions and Admissions: Reflections on 100,000 Admissions Decisions at Stanford* (Stanford, CA: Stanford University Press, 1995).

Rubenstone, Sally. *College Admissions: A Crash Course for Panicked Parents* (New York, NY: Arco, 1994).

Springer, Sally, John Reider, Marion Franck. *Admission Matters* (San Francisco, CA: Jossey-Bass, 2009).

Steinberg, Jacques. *The Gatekeepers* (New York, NY: Penguin Books, 2003).

Thacker, Lloyd (editor). *College Unranked* (Portland, OR: The Education Conservancy, 2004).

Van Buskirk, Peter. *Winning the College Admission Game: Strategies for Parents and Students* (Lawrenceville, NJ: Peterson's, 2007).

## Competitive Colleges

Antonoff, Steven. *The College Finder*, 3rd edition (Westford, MA: Wintergreen Orchard House, 2008).

Fiske, Edward B., *Fiske Guide to Colleges* (Naperville, IL: Sourcebooks Inc., annually updated).

Greene, Howard and Matthew Greene. *The Hidden Ivies: Thirty Colleges of Excellence* (New York, NY: Cliff Street Books, 2000).

Montauk, Richard and Krista Klein. *How to Get Into the Top Colleges* (Upper Saddle River, NJ: Prentice-Hall, 2006).

## Alternative Colleges

Mathews, Jay. *Harvard Schmarvard: Getting Beyond the Ivy League to the College That Is Best for You* (New York, NY: Three Rivers Press, 2003).

Pope, Loren. *Colleges That Change Lives: 40 Colleges You Should Know about Even if You're Not a Straight-A Student* (New York, NY: Penguin Books, 2000).

Pope, Loren. *Looking Beyond the Ivy League: Finding the College That Is Right for You* (New York, NY: Penguin Books, 1995).

## College Visits

Spencer, Janet and Sandra Maleson. *Visiting College Campuses* (New York, NY: Princeton Review Publishing, 2004).

## The Essay

Muchnick, Cynthia and Mark Stewart. *The Best College Admission Essays* (New York, NY: Peterson's, 2004).

## Summers and Scholarships

Peterson's *Scholarship Grants and Prizes* (New York, NY: Thomson Peterson's, 2005).

Peterson's *Summer Opportunities for Kids and Teens* (New York, NY: Thomson Peterson's, 2005).

Peterson's *Summer Study Abroad* (New York, NY: Thomson Peterson's, 2005).

Schwebel, Sara. *Yale Daily News Guide to Summer Programs* (New York, NY: Simon & Schuster, 2004).

## Financial Aid

O'Shaughnessey, Lynn. *The College Solution* (Upper Saddle River, NJ: FT Press, 2008).

The College Board. *Getting Financial Aid* (New York, NY: The College Board, updated annually).

## Resources for Students with Learning Disabilities and Attention-Deficit/Hyperactivity Disorder

Koehler, Michael. *Counseling Secondary Students with Learning Disabilities* (West Nyack, NY: Center for Applied Research in Education, 1998).

Kravets, Marybeth. *The K & W Guide to Colleges for Students with Learning Disabilities* (New York, NY: Princeton Review, 2007).

Lipkin, Midge. *The College Sourcebook for Students with Learning and Developmental Differences* (Westford, MA: Wintergreen Orchard Press, 2009).

## SAT Prep

Moshan, Michael. *Rock the SAT* (New York, NY: McGraw-Hill, 2006).

## Transition to College for Parents

Kastner, Laura and Jennifer Wyatt. *The Launching Years: Strategies for Parenting from Senior Year to College Life* (New York, NY: Three Rivers Press, 2002).

Savage, Marjorie. *You're on Your Own (But I'm Here if You Need Me): Mentoring Your Child During the College Years* (New York, NY: Fireside, 2003).

## Online Resources

### *College Admission Profiles*

Provides helpful information to college-bound students, school counselors, and college guidance specialists.

*www.college-admission-profiles.com*

### *College Board*

Use the College Board's website to register for the College Scholarship Service Financial Aid Profile. The CSS Profile is the application used to apply for nonfederal financial aid.

*www.collegeboard.com*

### College Confidential

Much of the information on CC is user-generated content. There are many official college admission office representatives who participate along with other school counselors, teachers, and independent college consultants.
*www.collegeconfidential.com*

### College Scholarships, Colleges, and Online Degrees

This is an all-inclusive website that offers free scholarship searches.
*www.college-scholarships.com*

### Cynthia Clumeck Muchnick, MA

Check this website for information on author's background and services as well as contact information to arrange a speaking engagement or workshop.
*www.cynthiamuchnick.com*

### English Grammar Online

This is a useful site where you can learn how to write English texts.
*www.ego4u.com*

### Enrichment Alley

Get a list of summer programs, school year enrichment, and gap-year programs.
*www.enrichmentalley.com*

### FastAid

This is a free online scholarship database. It also includes financial aid information and gives you help in understanding the SAR. The Student Aid Report (SAR) is the financial aid package offered by schools.
*www.fastaid.com*

### FastWeb

Use this free scholarship search program to search for information on more than 1.3 million scholarships, student loans, financial aid, etc. Information on local and federal aid, a "Q and A" section, a financial aid timeline, and a glossary are also included.

*www.fastweb.com*

### FinAid

Check out this comprehensive free resource for objective and unbiased information, advice and tools about financial aid, including a financial aid "calculator."

*www.finaid.org*

### Financial Aid Assistance

Here is another all-inclusive website that offers financial aid advice.

*www.financialaid4you.com*

### Free Application for Federal Student Aid

Find online registration for the Free Application for Federal Student Aid (FAFSA) along with answers to frequently asked questions about the financial aid process.

*www.fafsa.ed.gov*

### Fresch Free Scholarship Search

Fresch offers free scholarship search. The site also covers financial aid, including a comparison of various loan programs. Special features include a section on scholarship scams and links to other sites of interest with a good description of each.

*www.freschinfo.com*

### Guaranteed College Scholarships

You will find a list of scholarships offered by specific colleges to students with a good combination of SAT scores and GPA. The amount of the scholarships and the level of scores and grades needed to qualify vary widely.

*www.guaranteed-scholarships.com*

### Independent Educational Consultant Association (IECA)

This is a listing of members of the Independent Educational Consultant Association. The site provides a prescreened, legitimate college counselor search as well as pertinent articles and blogs.

*www.iecaonline.com*

### Kaarme Scholarships

This is a completely free site and requires no login to find scholarship information. It is also helpful as a site that exposes deceptive practices by scholarship and online college sites and supporters of independent college consulting.

*www.kaarme.com*

### Managing College Cost

Find a complete understanding of the college financial aid/costs road map.

*www.managingcollegecost.com*

### Modern Language Association

Check out this go-to source for proper English grammar and usage.

*www.mla.org*

### My College Options
Find a free college-planning program.
*www.mycollegeoptions.org*

### National Association for College Admissions Counseling (NACAC)
Provides articles, resources, and current events pertaining to admission and college counseling fields, trends, and current events in general. Website has an extensive LISTSERV open to members.
*www.nacacnet.org*

### National Association for Fair and Open Testing
This is a nonprofit advocacy organization dedicated to preventing the misuse of standardized tests and offering a growing list of schools that are standardized-test optional.
*www.fairtest.org*

# STUDY CALENDAR

| Time | Activity |
|------|----------|
| 8–9:00 | |
| 9–10:00 | |
| 10–11:00 | |
| 11–12:00 | |
| 12–1:00 | |
| 1–2:00 | |
| 2–3:00 | |
| 3–4:00 | |
| 4–5:00 | |
| 5–6:00 | |
| 6–7:00 | |
| 7–8:00 | |
| 8–9:00 | |
| 9–10:00 | |

| Time | Activity |
|------|----------|
| 8–9:00 | |
| 9–10:00 | |
| 10–11:00 | |
| 11–12:00 | |
| 12–1:00 | |
| 1–2:00 | |
| 2–3:00 | |
| 3–4:00 | |
| 4–5:00 | |
| 5–6:00 | |
| 6–7:00 | |
| 7–8:00 | |
| 8–9:00 | |
| 9–10:00 | |

| Time | Activity |
|------|----------|
| 8–9:00 | |
| 9–10:00 | |
| 10–11:00 | |
| 11–12:00 | |
| 12–1:00 | |
| 1–2:00 | |
| 2–3:00 | |
| 3–4:00 | |
| 4–5:00 | |
| 5–6:00 | |
| 6–7:00 | |
| 7–8:00 | |
| 8–9:00 | |
| 9–10:00 | |

| Time | Activity |
|------|----------|
| 8–9:00 | |
| 9–10:00 | |
| 10–11:00 | |
| 11–12:00 | |
| 12–1:00 | |
| 1–2:00 | |
| 2–3:00 | |
| 3–4:00 | |
| 4–5:00 | |
| 5–6:00 | |
| 6–7:00 | |
| 7–8:00 | |
| 8–9:00 | |
| 9–10:00 | |

# THURSDAY

| Time | Activity |
|------|----------|
| 8–9:00 | |
| 9–10:00 | |
| 10–11:00 | |
| 11–12:00 | |
| 12–1:00 | |
| 1–2:00 | |
| 2–3:00 | |
| 3–4:00 | |
| 4–5:00 | |
| 5–6:00 | |
| 6–7:00 | |
| 7–8:00 | |
| 8–9:00 | |
| 9–10:00 | |

**FRIDAY**

| Time | Activity |
|------|----------|
| 8–9:00 | |
| 9–10:00 | |
| 10–11:00 | |
| 11–12:00 | |
| 12–1:00 | |
| 1–2:00 | |
| 2–3:00 | |
| 3–4:00 | |
| 4–5:00 | |
| 5–6:00 | |
| 6–7:00 | |
| 7–8:00 | |
| 8–9:00 | |
| 9–10:00 | |

| Time | Activity |
|------|----------|
| 8–9:00 | |
| 9–10:00 | |
| 10–11:00 | |
| 11–12:00 | |
| 12–1:00 | |
| 1–2:00 | |
| 2–3:00 | |
| 3–4:00 | |
| 4–5:00 | |
| 5–6:00 | |
| 6–7:00 | |
| 7–8:00 | |
| 8–9:00 | |
| 9–10:00 | |

# NOTES

# NOTES

# INDEX

# ABOUT THE AUTHORS

**Cynthia Clumeck Muchnick, MA** (*www.cynthiamuchnick.com*), is an accomplished educator, author, public speaker, and educational consultant. She is a graduate of Stanford University, worked as an Assistant Director of Admission for both the Illinois Institute of Technology and the University of Chicago, taught SAT prep for Princeton Review, and was a high school history teacher. Cindy privately counsels eighth- through twelfth-grade students. She assists with class selection, study and writing skills, extracurricular and summer activity planning, test prep, and college admission. She presents seminars and workshops on succeeding in high school and college, writing college essays, and applying to college. Cindy is the author of *The Everything® Guide to Study Skills* and coauthor of *The Best College Admission Essays*. *Straight-A Study Skills* is her seventh book. She lives in Newport Beach, CA, with her husband and four children.

**Justin Muchnick** attends Phillips Academy Andover in Massachusetts and has been practicing "Straight-A Study Skills" his entire life. He is currently the youngest journalist for *The Bootleg* (*www.scout.com*), Stanford University's sports' news website, where he publishes articles about college football. In addition, his work has appeared in multiple literary magazines. Justin's academic interests include reading, writing, Latin, modern American history, politics, and foreign policy.